7-DAY QUILTS

If you have thought making a quilt to be too daunting a task, this is the book for you!

Because we thought quilt making was considered a chore, we tended to limit it to old grandmothers who seemed to have the spare time to cut and piece those little bits of fabric. Today's grandmother, however, is much too busy working out in the gym to spend time cutting, piecing, and sewing little bits of fabric back together. She—like all of us—wants to create a beautiful quilt, but she needs fast and easy methods.

And, here they are!

The quilts in this collection were designed and made by two wonderful ladies, who are busy, but never too busy to create a quilt: Lee Grover and Christina Jensen. Both ladies sport advanced degrees from prestigious Eastern colleges. Lee has worked for many years in science laboratories, where she's helped to develop drugs that may have saved the lives of countless newborns. Christina has worked in Hollywood and New York writing screen plays and TV shows. Both women, however, have been secret quilters, who have made many quilts for friends and relatives. Their busy lives mandated that they develop quick methods for quilt making. Once the two women met and started to share their love of quilting, there was no stopping them. Hollywood and the scientific world may have lost two outstanding women; the quilt world—I'm sure you will agree—gained two of the finest.

Fast and easy is the name of the game! Dust off your sewing machine, get out your rotary cutter, your cutting mat, and that fabric you've collected for "Someday I'll have the time to make a quilt." That time is now; in just seven days, you can create any one of the quilts in this collection. Your friends and relatives will be truly amazed!

CONTENTS

Jitterbugs 3

Four-Patch Weave 10

Let's Play Ball 16

Nine-Patch Novelty 24

Roses Galore 30

Jungle Fever 36

Star-Crossed Garden 43

Diamonds & Nosegays 50

General Quiltmaking Instructions 57

Carol Wilson Mansfield, Art Director

James Jaeger, Photography

Graphic Solutions inc-chgo, Book Design

Produced by The Creative Partners™

©2004 by Leisure Arts, Inc, 5701 Ranch Drive, Little Rock, AR 72223-9633. All rights reserved. This publication is protected under federal copyright laws. Reproduction or distribution of this publication or any other Leisure Arts publication, including publications which are out of print, is prohibited unless specifically authorized. This includes, but is not limited to, any form of reproduction or distribution on or through the Internet, including posting, scanning, or e-mail transmission.

JITTERBUGS

Designed by Lee Grover

Finished Quilt Size 54 1/2" x 74 1/2"
Finished Block Size 12" x 12"
Number of Blocks 15

MATERIALS

Lime-green print. . . . . 1/2 yard
Pink tonal . . . . 3/4 yard
Yellow print . . . . 1 yard
Purple print . . . . 1 1/2 yards
Allover novelty print . . . . . 2 3/8 yards
Backing . . . . 60" x 80"
Batting. . . . . 60" x 80"
Coordinating thread
Rotary-cutting tools

CUTTING INSTRUCTIONS

Lime-green print
- 2 strips 7 1/4" x fabric width; cut into 32-2 1/4" x 7 1/4" B rectangles

Pink tonal
- 1 strip 3 3/4" x fabric width; cut into 8-3 3/4" squares; cut each square on both diagonals to make 32 C triangles
- 1 strip 1 3/4" x fabric width; cut into 16-1 3/4" x 3" G rectangles

- 4-2 1/2" x 2 1/2" L squares
- 7 strips 2 1/4" x fabric width for binding

Yellow print
- 2 strips 7 1/4" x fabric width; cut into 8-7 1/4" A squares
- 5 strips 1 3/4" x fabric width; cut into 32-1 3/4" H squares, 4-1 3/4" x 6 1/2" I rectangles, 12-1 3/4" x 10" J strips and 4-1 3/4" x 5 1/4" K rectangles

Purple print
- 3 strips 5 5/8" x fabric width; cut into 16-5 5/8" squares; cut each square in half on 1 diagonal to make 32 D triangles
- 4 strips 5 1/4" x fabric width; cut into 28-5 1/4" F squares
- 5 M/N strips 2 1/2" by fabric width

Allover novelty print
Note: Fabric used was a directional print.

- 3 strips 12 1/2" x fabric width; cut into 7-12 1/2" E squares
- 4 O strips 6 1/2" by fabric width
- 3 P strips 4 1/2" by fabric width

JITTERBUGS

PIECING THE FRAMED A BLOCKS

1. Sew B to opposite sides of A; press seams toward B. Repeat with all A squares.

2. Sew C to opposite ends of each remaining B (Diagram 1); press seams toward B.

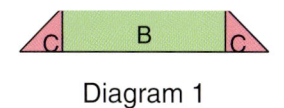

Diagram 1

3. Sew a B-C unit to the remaining sides of A; press seams toward A (Diagram 2).

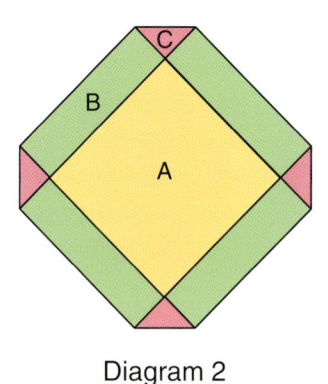

Diagram 2

4. Sew D to each side of the pieced unit to complete a block; press seams toward D (Diagram 3). Repeat for eight Framed A blocks.

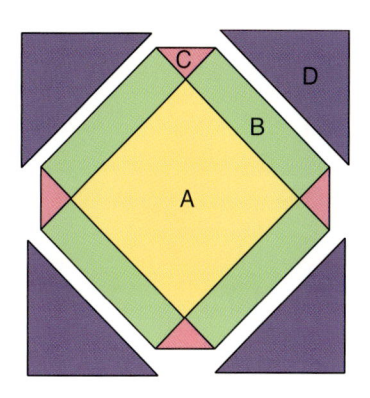

Diagram 3

PIECING THE SNOWBALL E BLOCKS

1. Draw a diagonal line from corner to corner on the wrong side of each F square.

2. Place an F square on each corner of an E square (Diagram 4). Stitch on the marked line, trim seams to 1/4" and press F to the right side to complete a block; repeat for seven Snowball E blocks.

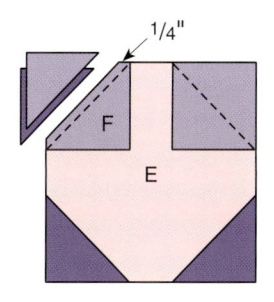

Diagram 4

5

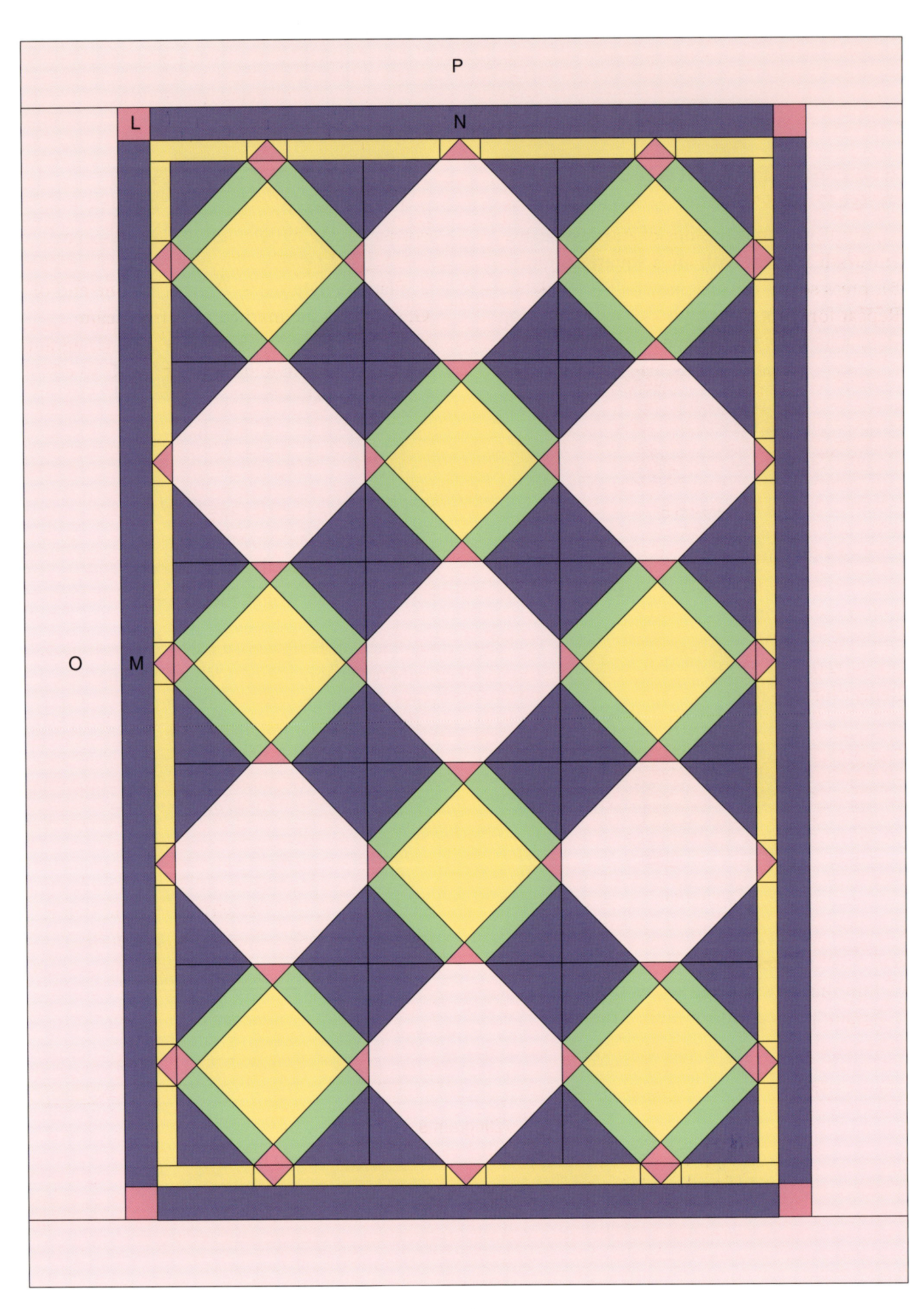

Jitterbugs
Assembly Diagram 54 1/2" x 74 1/2"

ASSEMBLING THE QUILT CENTER

1. Join two Framed A blocks and one Snowball E block to make a row (Diagram 5); press seams toward Snowball E block. Repeat for three rows.

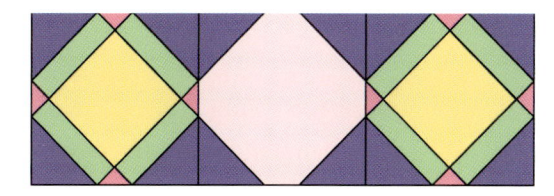

Diagram 5

2. Join two Snowball E blocks and one Framed A block to make a row (Diagram 6); press seams toward Snowball E blocks. Repeat for two rows.

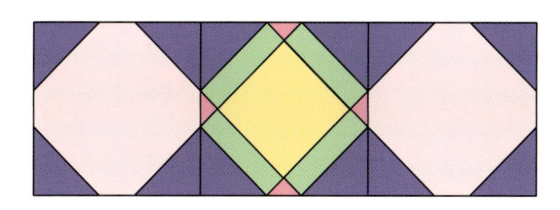

Diagram 6

3. Join the rows referring to the Assembly Diagram; press seams in one direction.

ADDING BORDERS

1. Draw a diagonal line from corner to corner on the wrong side of each H square.

2. Place H right sides together on one end of G, stitch on the marked line, trim seam allowance to 1/4" and press H open (Diagram 7); repeat on the remaining end of G to complete one H-G unit. Repeat to make 16 units.

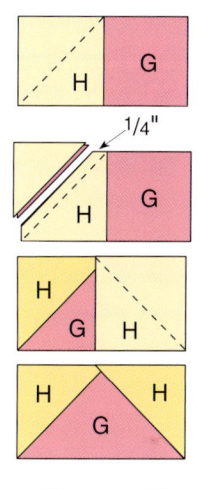

Diagram 7

3. Join five H-G units with four J and two K pieces to make a side strip (Diagram 8); repeat for two side strips. Press seams toward J and K.

Diagram 8

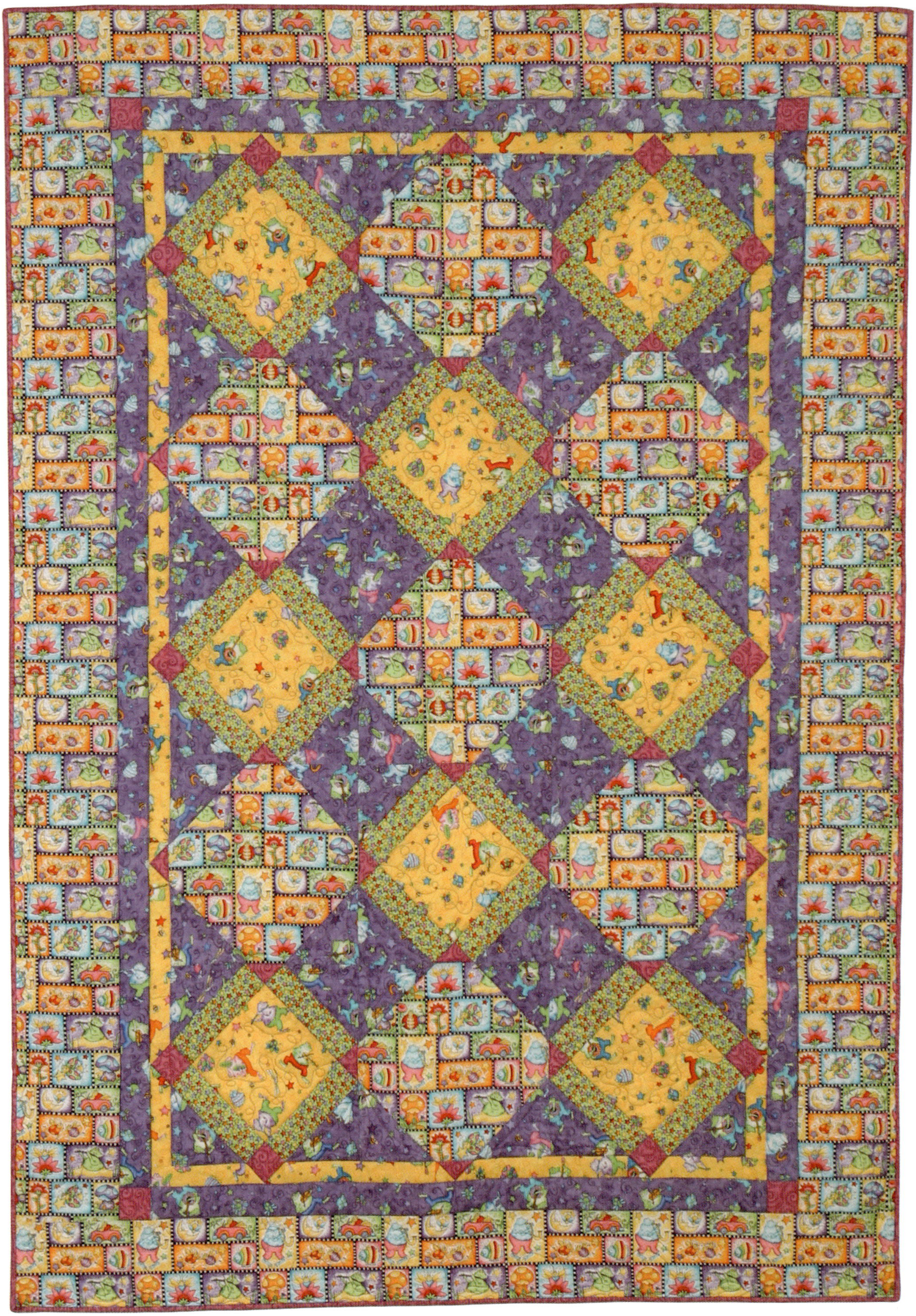

4. Sew a side strip to opposite long sides of the quilt center; press seams toward pieced strips.

5. Join three H-G units with two J and two I pieces to make a top strip (Diagram 9); repeat for a bottom strip. Press seams toward J and I.

6. Sew strips to the top and bottom of the quilt center; press seams toward pieced strips.

7. Join M/N border strips on short ends to make a long strip; cut into two 63" M strips and two 39" N strips.

8. Sew an M strip to opposite long sides of the quilt center; press seams toward M.

9. Sew an L square to each end of each N strip; press seams toward N. Sew the L-N strips to the top and bottom of the quilt center; press seams toward L-N.

10. Join the O strips on short ends to make a long strip; cut into two 67" O strips. Sew an O strip to opposite long sides of the quilt center; press seams toward O.

11. Join the P strips on short ends to make a long strip; cut into two 55" P strips. Sew a P strip to the top and bottom of the quilt center; press seams toward P.

Diagram 9

FINISHING THE QUILT

1. Layer and baste quilt top for quilting method of choice referring to General Quiltmaking Instructions.

2. Quilt as desired.

3. Trim batting and backing even with top.

4. Bind quilt with pink tonal binding strips referring to General Quiltmaking Instructions.

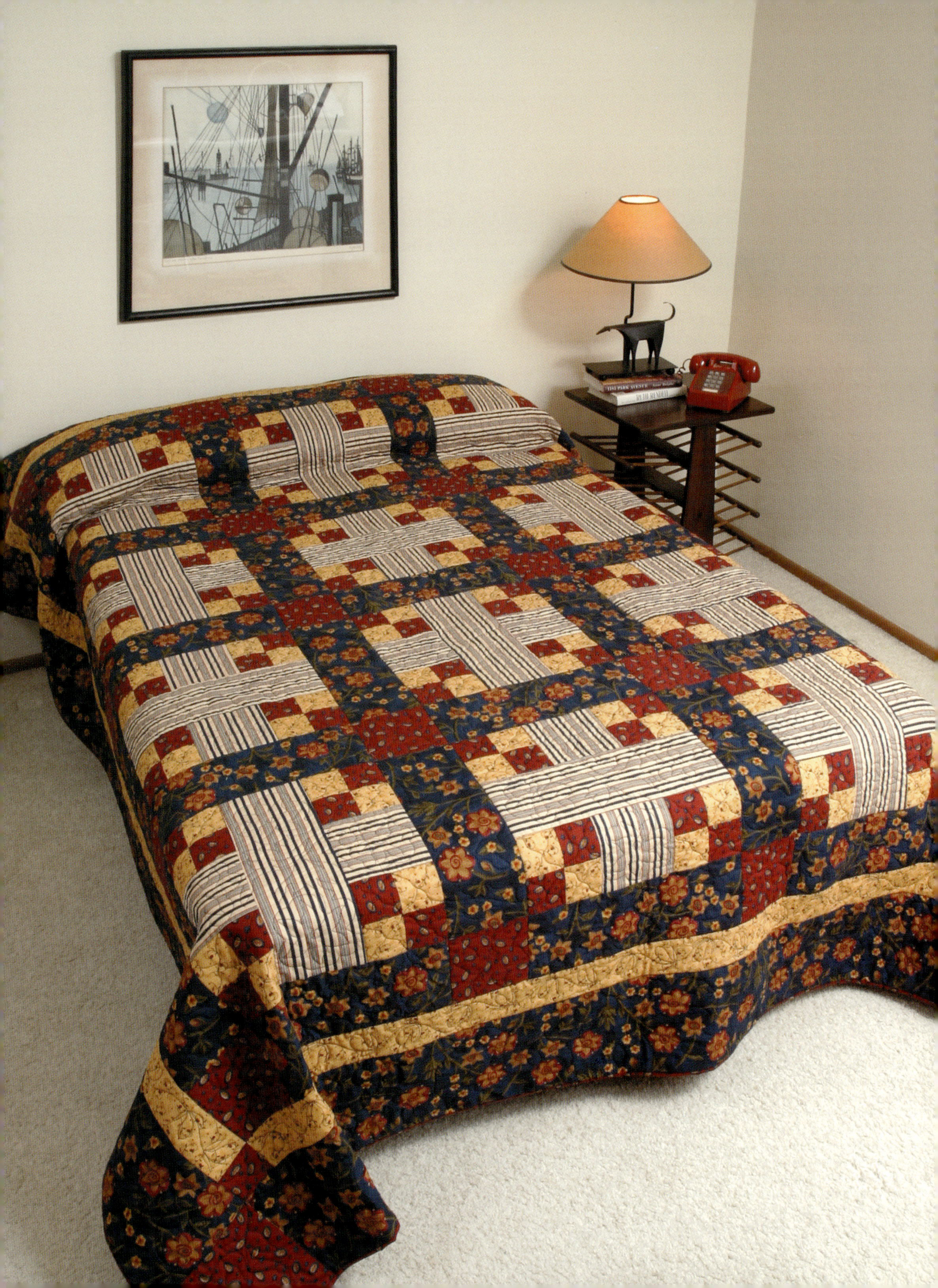

FOUR-PATCH WEAVE

Designed by Christina Jensen

Finished Quilt Size 85" x 105"
Finished Block Size 15" x 15"
Number of Blocks 12

MATERIALS

Note: All fabrics from the Old Blooms collection by Pat Sloan for P&B Textiles

Blue/red/tan stripe . . . . 1 2/3 yards
Small red print . . . . 2 1/4 yards
Gold print . . . . 3 1/4 yards
Navy floral . . . . 4 7/8 yards
Backing . . . . 91" x 111"
Batting . . . . 91" x 111"
Coordinating thread
Rotary-cutting tools

CUTTING INSTRUCTIONS

Blue/red/tan stripe
- 4 strips 5 1/2" x fabric width; cut into 24-5 1/2" C squares
- 2 strips 15 1/2" x fabric width; cut into 12-5 1/2" x 15 1/2" D rectangles

Small red print
- 7 A strips 3" x fabric width
- 3 strips 5 1/2" x fabric width; cut into 20-5 1/2" F squares
- 4-3" I squares
- 4-8" L squares
- 10 strips 2 1/4" x fabric width for binding

Gold print
- 7 B strips 3" x fabric width
- 2 G strips 3" x 85 1/2" along length of fabric
- 2 H strips 3" x 65 1/2" along length of fabric

Navy floral
- 5 strips 15 1/2" x fabric width; cut into 31-5 1/2" x 15 1/2" E rectangles
- 2 J strips 8" x 90 1/2" along length of fabric
- 2 K strips 8" x 70 1/2" along length of fabric

PIECING THE BLOCKS

1. Sew an A strip to a B strip along length with right sides together; press seam toward A. Repeat to make seven A-B strip sets.

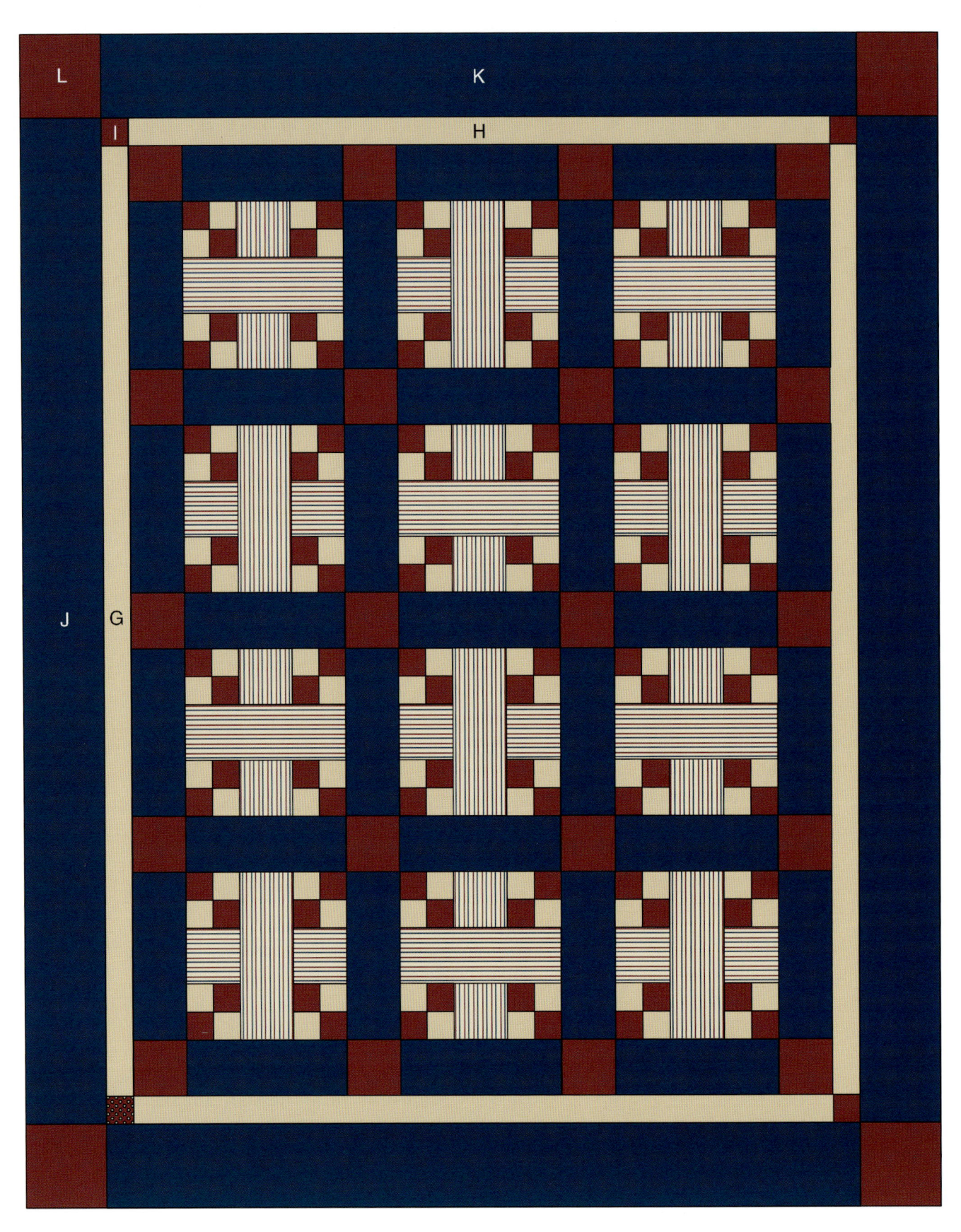

Four-Patch Weave
Assembly Diagram 85" x 105"

FOUR-PATCH WEAVE

2. Cut 96-3" A-B segments from strip sets (Diagram 1).

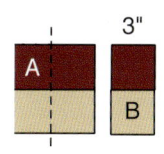

Diagram 1

3. Join two A-B segments to make a Four-Patch unit (Diagram 2); press seam in one direction. Repeat for 48 units.

Diagram 2

4. Sew a C square between two Four-Patch units (Diagram 3); press seams toward C. Repeat for 24 pieced strips.

Diagram 3

5. Sew a D rectangle between two pieced strips to complete a block (Diagram 4); press seams toward D. Repeat to make 12 blocks.

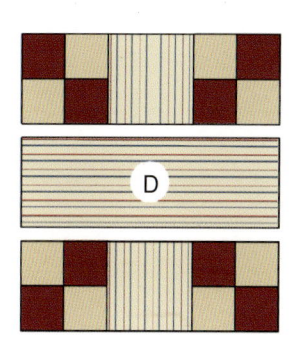

Diagram 4

ASSEMBLING THE TOP

Note: Refer to the Assembly Diagram as needed for the following instructions.

1. Join three blocks with four E rectangles to make a block row (Diagram 5); press seams toward E. Repeat to make four block rows.

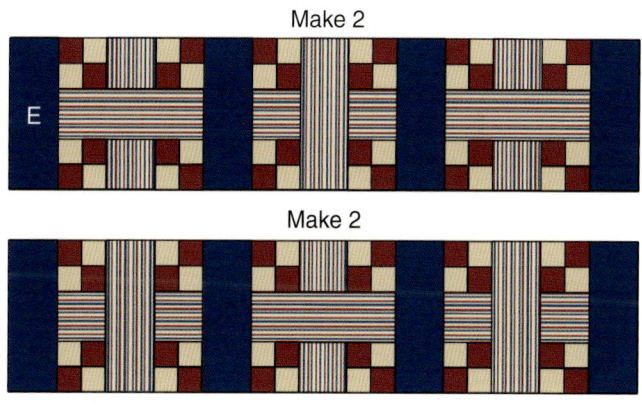

Make 2

Make 2

Diagram 5

2. Join three E rectangles with four F squares to make a sashing row (Diagram 6); press seams toward E. Repeat to make five sashing rows.

Diagram 6

14

FOUR-PATCH WEAVE

3. Join the block and sashing rows to complete the pieced center, beginning and ending with a sashing row.

4. Sew a G strip to opposite sides; press seams toward strips.

5. Sew an I square to each end of each H strip; press seams toward H. Sew a strip to the top and bottom; press seams toward strips.

6. Sew a J strip to opposite sides; press seams toward strips.

7. Sew an L square to each end of each K strip; press seams toward K. Sew a strip to the top and bottom; press seams toward K and L strips to complete the top.

FINISHING THE QUILT

1. Layer and baste top, batting and backing for quilting method of choice referring to General Quiltmaking Instructions.

2. Quilt as desired.

3. Trim batting and backing even with top.

4. Bind quilt with small red print binding strips referring to General Quiltmaking Instructions.

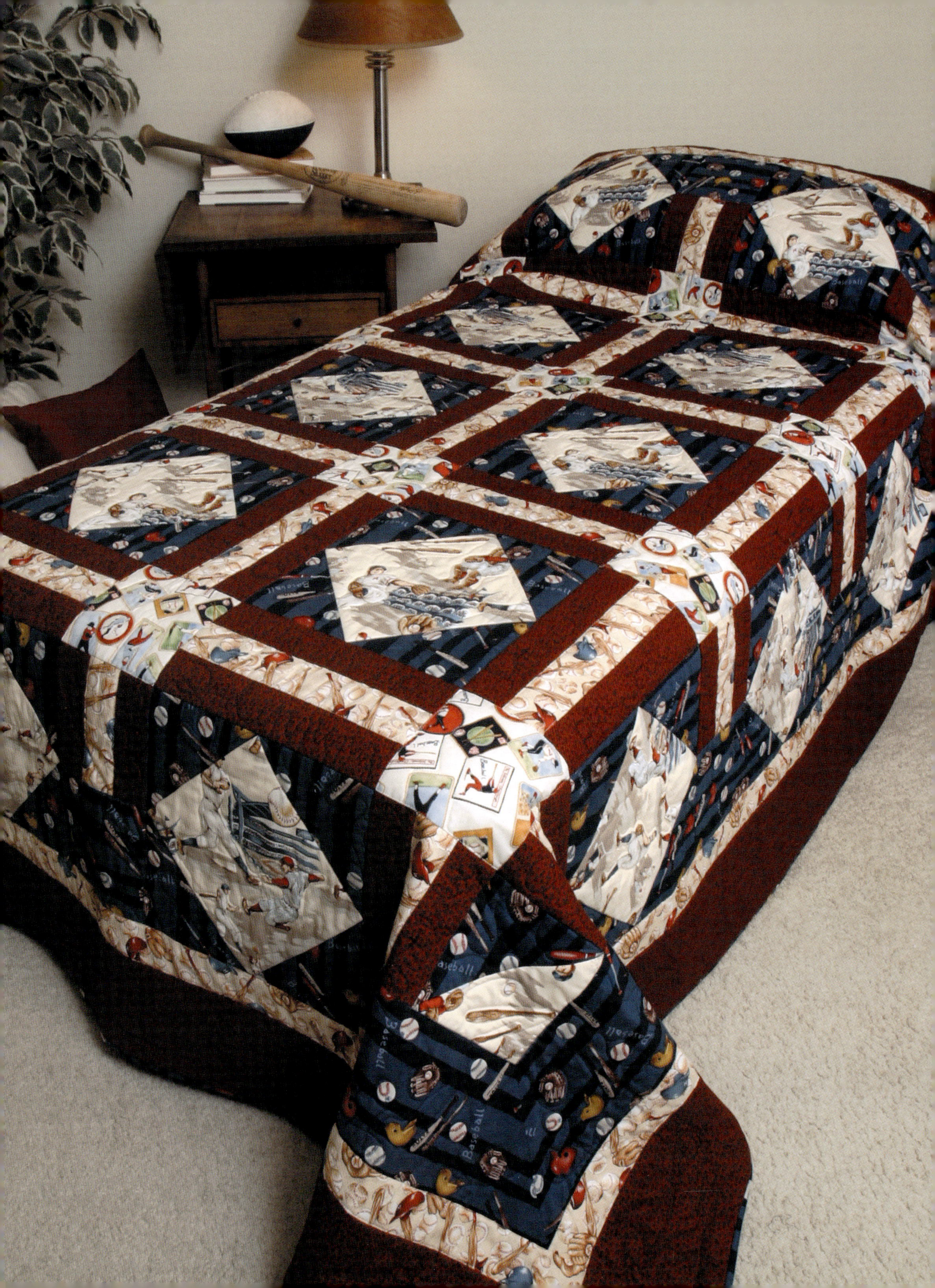
Baseball

LET'S PLAY BALL

Designed by Lee Grover

Finished Quilt Size 82" x 100"
Finished Block Size 12" x 12"
Number of Blocks 16

MATERIALS

Note: All fabrics from the Vintage Sports collection from RJR Fabrics

Small motif print . . . . 1/2 yard
Glove print . . . . 1 1/4 yards
Large motif print . . . . 2 1/8 yards
Red print. . . . . 3 yards
Blue stripe/print . . . . 4 yards
Backing . . . . 86" x 106"
Batting. . . . . 86" x 106"
Coordinating thread
Rotary-cutting tools

CUTTING INSTRUCTIONS

Small motif print
- 2 strips 6 1/2" x fabric width; cut into 12-6 1/2" C squares

Glove print
- 8 D/E strips 2 1/2" x fabric width
- 8 I/J strips 2 1/2" x fabric width

LARGE MOTIF PRINT
Note: The fabric used was a directional print.

- 6 strips 12 1/2" x fabric width; cut into 16-12 1/2" A squares
- 2-6 7/8" squares; cut each square on 1 diagonal to make 4 F triangles

Red print
- 16 D/E strips 2 1/2" x fabric width
- 9 K/L strips 6 1/2" x fabric width

Blue stripe/print
Note: A print fabric is preferable to a stripe fabric in this pattern; when using a stripe, special cutting steps apply to keep the stripe flowing in the right direction.

- 12 strips 6 1/2" x fabric width; cut into 70-6 1/2" B squares
- 2 strips 18 1/2" x fabric width; cut into 8-6 1/2" x 18 1/2" H strips and 2-6 7/8" squares; cut each square on 1 diagonal to make 4 G triangles
- 9 strips 2 1/4" x fabric width for binding

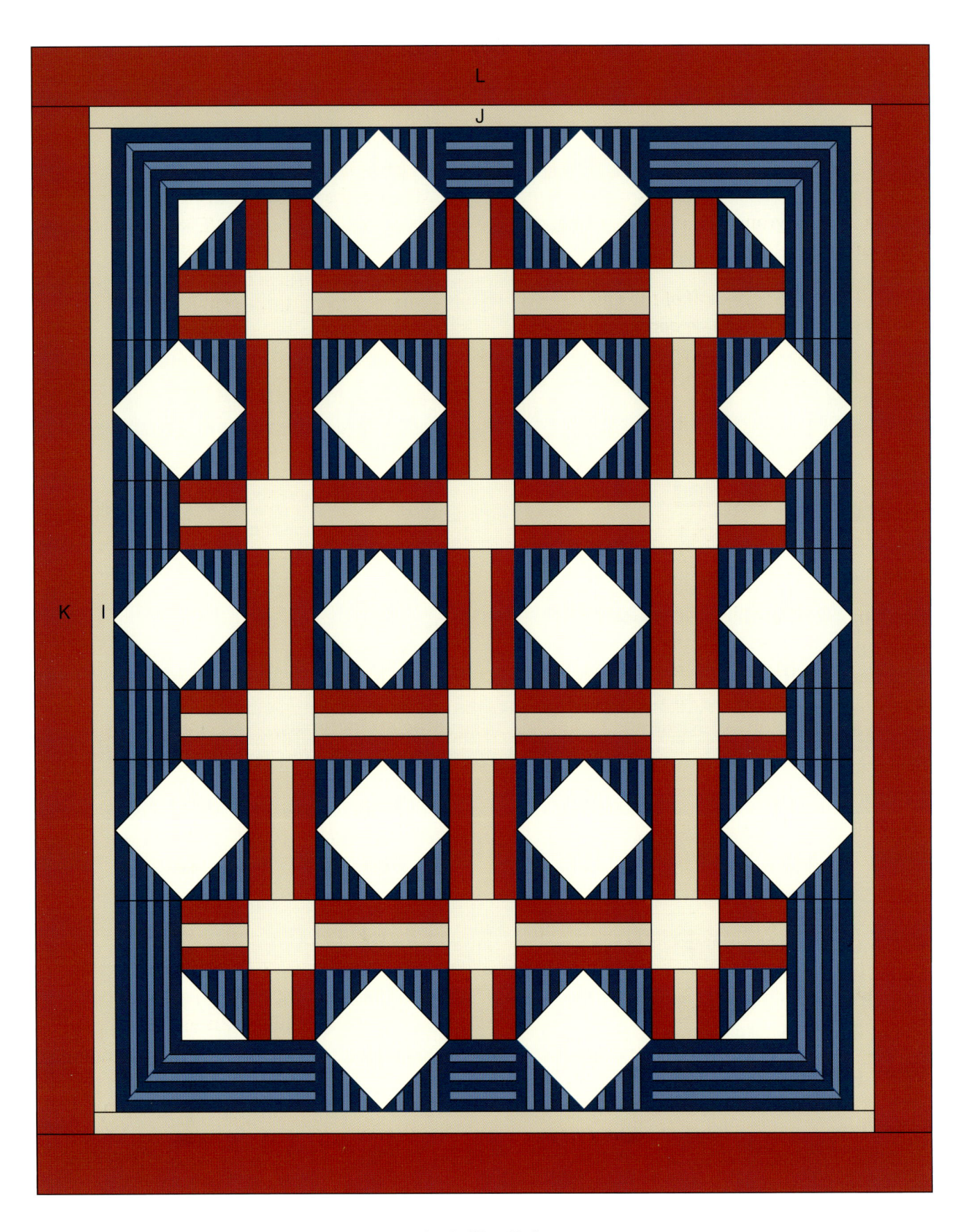

Let's Play Ball
Assembly Diagram 82" x 100"

LET'S PLAY BALL

PIECING THE BLOCKS

1. Set aside six B squares for borders.

2. Draw a diagonal line from corner to corner on the wrong side of each remaining B square.

Note: If using a stripe, half of the squares should have lines drawn on opposite corners (Diagram 1) in order to keep the stripe in an upright position on all corners of the completed blocks.

Diagram 1

3. Place a B square right sides together on one corner of A; stitch on marked line (Diagram 2). Trim seam allowance to 1/4" and press B open; repeat on each corner of A to complete one block. Repeat for 16 blocks.

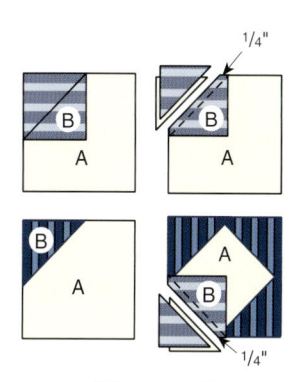

Diagram 2

PIECING THE D AND E UNITS

1. Sew a glove print D/E strip between two red print D-E strips along length with right sides together; press seams toward red print strips. Repeat for eight D/E strip sets.

2. Cut D/E strip sets into 14-6 1/2" D units and 17-12 1/2" E units (Diagram 3).

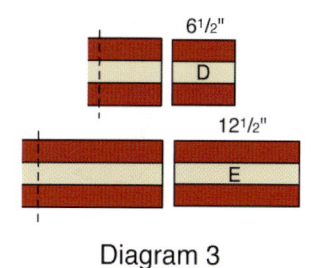

Diagram 3

ASSEMBLING THE QUILT CENTER

Note: If using a stripe fabric, refer to the Assembly Diagram for positioning of stripes when joining pieces.

1. Join four pieced blocks with three E units to make a row (Diagram 4); repeat for three block rows. Press seams toward E.

Block row

Diagram 4

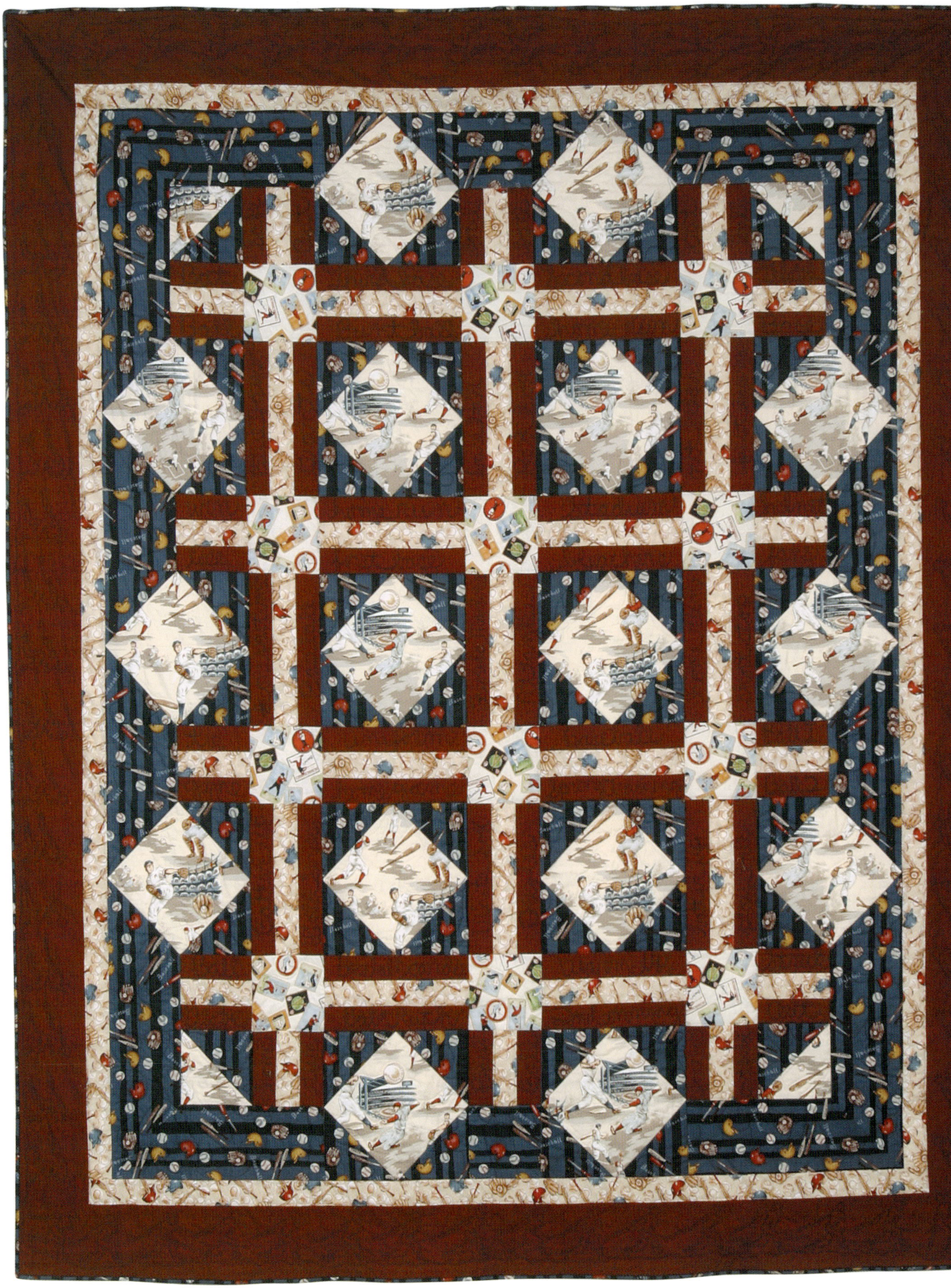

LET'S PLAY BALL

2. Join two D units with three C squares and two E units to make a D-C-E row (Diagram 5); repeat for four D-C-E rows. Press seams toward D and E units.

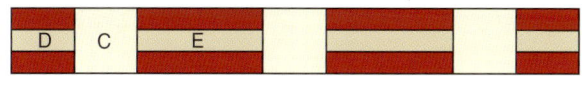

Diagram 5

3. Add B to each end of two D-C-E rows to make sashing rows; press seams toward B (Diagram 6).

Sashing row

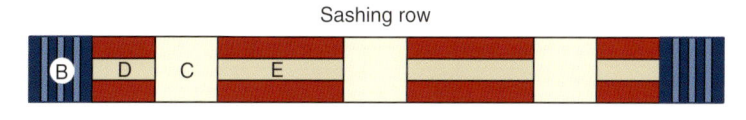

Diagram 6

4. Sew F to G along the diagonal (Diagram 7); press seam toward G. Repeat for four F-G units.

Diagram 7

5. Sew an F-G unit to a D unit (Diagram 8); repeat for two units and two reversed units. Press seams toward the D units.

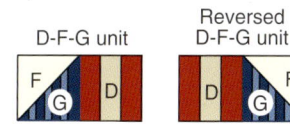

D-F-G unit   Reversed D-F-G unit

Diagram 8

6. Sew an D-F-G unit to H, stopping stitching at the end of the seam allowance (Diagram 9); press seam toward H. Repeat for two H units and two reversed H units (Diagram 10).

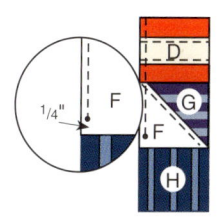

Diagram 9

H unit   Reversed H unit
Make 2   Make 2

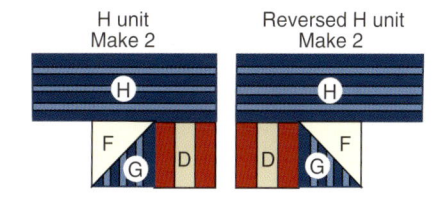

Diagram 10

Note: The excess H left at the ends of the pieced units is required for the mitered corner seam.

7. Sew a D unit to B (Diagram 11); press seam toward B. Repeat for two B-D units.

Diagram 11

LET'S PLAY BALL

8. Join two pieced blocks with one H unit, one reversed H unit and one B-D unit (Diagram 12); press seams away from the pieced blocks. Add a D-C-E row (Diagram 13); press seams toward the D-C-E row.

Diagram 12

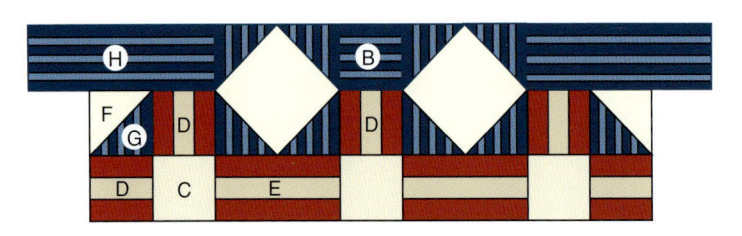

Diagram 13

9. Add an H strip to each end of the pieced unit to make an end row, mitering corners of H strips (Diagram 14); repeat for two end rows. Press seams toward H.

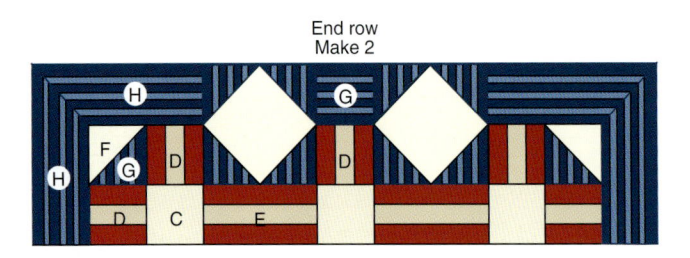

End row
Make 2

Diagram 14

10. Join the block rows with the sashing and end rows (Diagram 15).

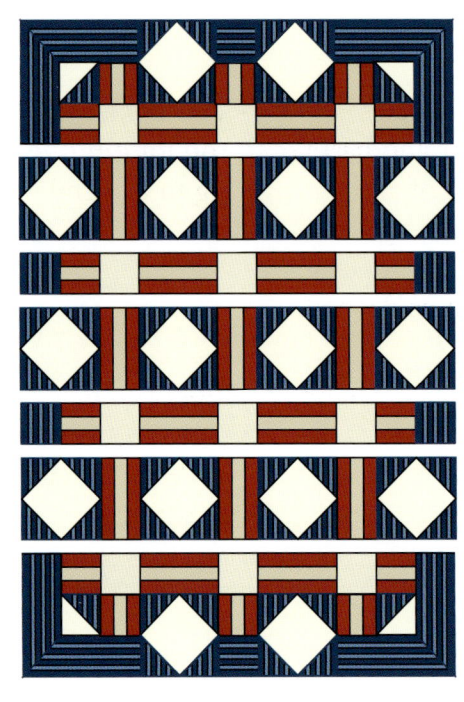

Diagram 15

ADDING BORDERS

1. Join the I/J strips on short ends to make one long strip; cut into two 84 1/2" I strips and two 70 1/2" J strips.

2. Sew an I strip to opposite sides and J strips to the top and bottom of the pieced center; press seams toward I and J.

3. Join the K/L strips on short ends to make one long strip; cut into two 88 1/2" K strips and two 82 1/2" L strips.

4. Sew a K strip to opposite sides and L strips to the top and bottom of the pieced center; press seams toward K and L.

FINISHING THE QUILT

1. Layer and baste quilt top for quilting method of choice referring to General Quiltmaking Instructions.

2. Quilt as desired.

3. Trim batting and backing even with top.

4. Bind quilt with blue stripe/print binding strips referring to General Quiltmaking Instructions.

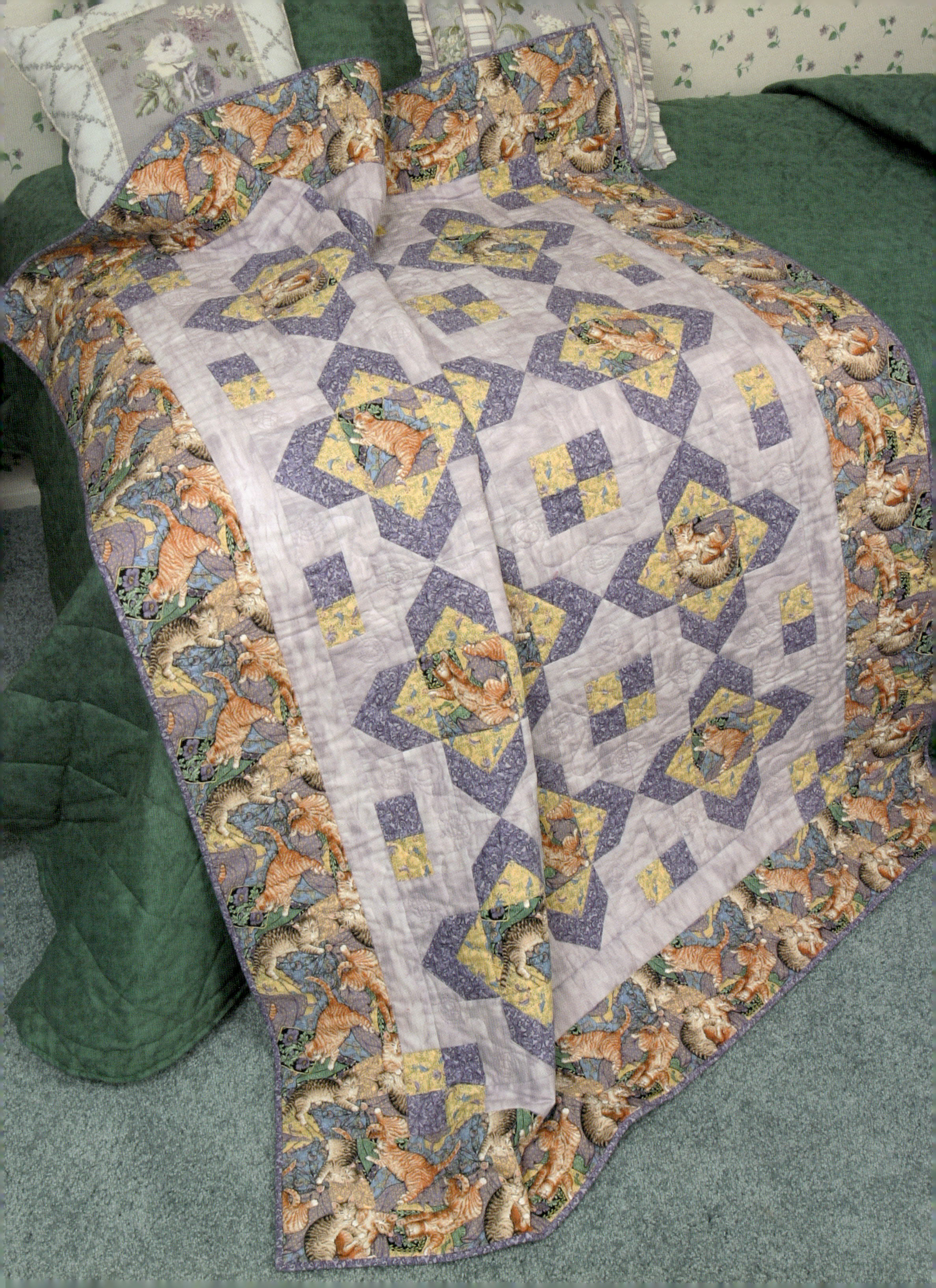

NINE-PATCH NOVELTY

Designed by Christina Jensen

Finished Quilt Size 52" x 64"
Finished Block Size 12" x 12"
Number of Blocks 12

MATERIALS

Note: *All fabrics from the Cat Napping collection from Robert Kaufman*

Yellow print . . . . 3/4 yard
Pale lilac mottled . . . . 1 5/8 yards
Purple print . . . . 1 5/8 yards
Cat novelty print . . . . 1 3/4 yards
Backing . . . . 58" x 70"
Batting . . . . 58" x 70"
Coordinating thread
Rotary-cutting tools

CUTTING INSTRUCTIONS

Yellow print
- 3 strips 4 1/2" x fabric width; cut into 48-2 1/2" x 4 1/2" C rectangles
- 2 G strips 2 1/2" x fabric width
- 6-2 1/2" H squares

Pale lilac mottled
- 4 G strips 2 1/2" x fabric width
- 2 J strips 2 1/2" x 44 1/2" along length of fabric
- 7 strips 2 1/2" x remaining fabric width; cut into 96-2 1/2" D squares
- 4 strips 4 1/2" x remaining fabric width; cut into 48-2 1/2" x 4 1/2" F rectangles
- 2 K strips 2 1/2" x 32 1/2"

Purple print
- 7 strips 2 1/2" x fabric width; cut into 96-2 1/2" B squares and 6-2 1/2" I squares
- 3 strips 4 1/2" x fabric width; cut into 48-2 1/2" x 4 1/2" E rectangles
- 2 G strips 2 1/2" x fabric width
- 6 strips 2 1/4" x fabric width for binding

Cat novelty print
- 4 L strips 6 1/2" x 52 1/2" along length of fabric
- 12-4 1/2" A squares with motif centered in square

Nine-Patch Novelty
Assembly Diagram 52" x 64"

NINE-PATCH NOVELTY

PIECING THE BLOCKS

1. Draw a diagonal line from corner to corner on the wrong side of all B and D squares.

2. Place B right sides together on one end of C, stitch on the marked line, trim seam allowance to 1/4" and press B open (Diagram 1); repeat on the remaining end of C to complete one B-C unit. Repeat to make 48 units.

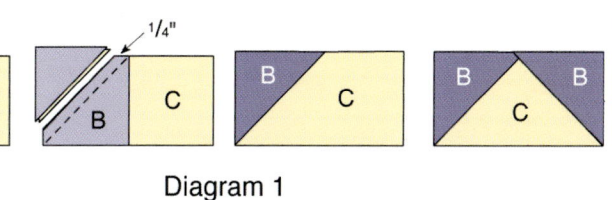

Diagram 1

3. Repeat step 2 with D and E pieces to make 48 D-E units (Diagram 2).

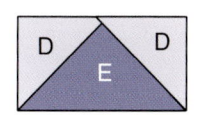

Diagram 2

4. Sew a B-C unit to a D-E unit (Diagram 3); press seam toward D-E. Repeat with all B-C and D-E units.

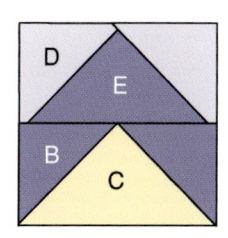

Diagram 3

5. Sew a purple G strip to a lilac G strip along length with right sides together; press seam toward purple. Repeat to make two purple strip sets.

6. Sew a yellow G strip to a lilac G strip along length with right sides together; press seam toward yellow. Repeat to make two yellow strip sets.

7. Cut each strip set into 2 1/2" segments to make 24 each purple and yellow G units (Diagram 4).

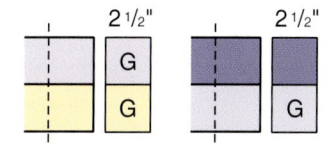

8. Sew F to a yellow G unit (Diagram 5); press seam toward F. Repeat with all yellow G units.

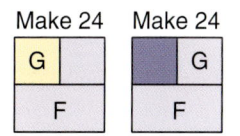

Diagram 5

9. Sew F to a purple G unit (Diagram 5); press seam toward F. Repeat with all purple G units.

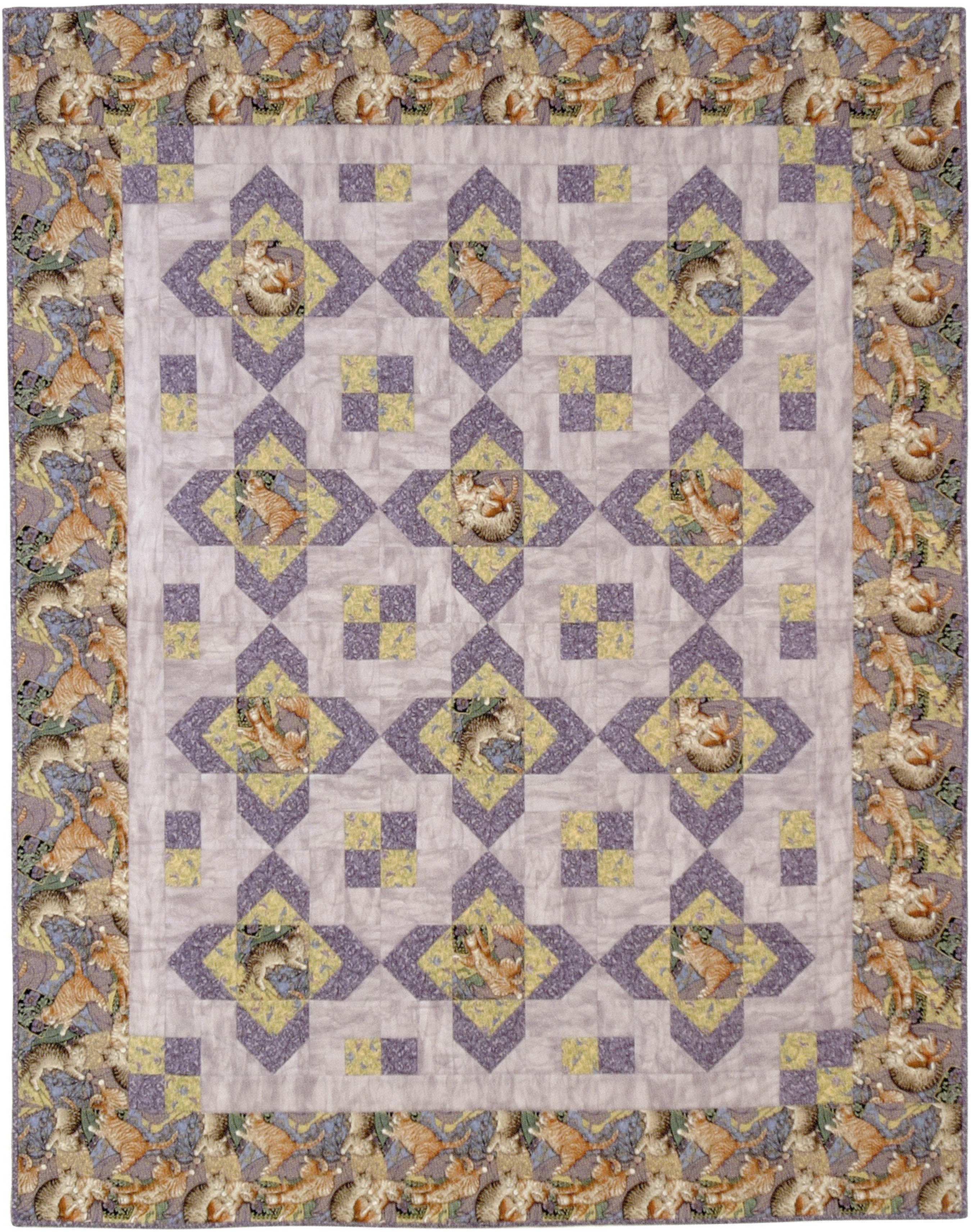

NINE-PATCH NOVELTY

10. Join units in rows with A and join rows to complete one block (Diagram 6); repeat to make 12 blocks.

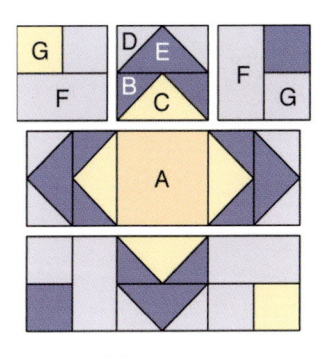

Diagram 6

ASSEMBLING THE TOP

Note: *Refer to the Assembly Diagram as needed for the following instructions.*

1. Join three blocks to make a row (Diagram 7); press seams in one direction. Repeat for four rows. Join the rows to complete the pieced center.

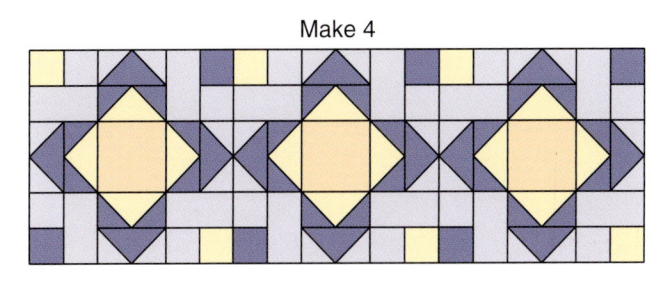

Make 4

Diagram 7

2. Sew an H square to one end of each J strip and an I square to the remaining end (Diagram 8); press seams as indicated. Sew a pieced strip to opposite long sides of the pieced center; press seams toward strips.

Diagram 8

3. Sew an I and H square to each end of each K strip (Diagram 9); press seams as indicated. Sew a pieced strip to the top and bottom of the pieced center; press seams toward strips.

Diagram 9

4. Sew an L strip to opposite long sides and then to the top and bottom of the pieced center to complete the top; press seams toward strips.

FINISHING THE QUILT

1. Layer and baste quilt top for quilting method of choice referring to General Quiltmaking Instructions.

2. Quilt as desired.

3. Trim batting and backing even with top.

4. Bind quilt with purple print binding strips referring to General Quiltmaking Instructions.

chantal delanoë
Aquarelles
DU 24 MARS AU 13 AVRIL 1987
Ouvert tous les jours de 11 h à 19 h - Dimanche compris

ROSES GALORE

Designed by Lee Grover

Finished Quilt Size 88" x 100"
Finished Block Size 8" x 8"
Number of Blocks 31

MATERIALS

Note: *All fabrics from the Donna's Roses fabric collection by Donna Dewberry for Springs Industries*

Vine print . . . . 1 1/2 yards
Green mottled. . . . . 2 1/2 yards
Cream tonal . . . . 2 5/8 yards
Large floral print. . . . . 4 yards
Backing . . . . 94" x 106"
Batting. . . . . 94" x 106"
Coordinating thread
Rotary-cutting tools

CUTTING INSTRUCTIONS

Vine print
- 11 strips 4 1/2" x fabric width; cut into 98-4 1/2" C squares

Green mottled
- 25 strips 2 1/2" x fabric width; cut into 392-2 1/2" B squares
- 10 strips 2 1/4" x fabric width for binding

Cream tonal
- 11 strips 4 1/2" x fabric width; cut into 98-4 1/2" D squares
- 14 E/F/G strips 2 1/2" x by fabric width

Large floral print
- 7 strips 8 1/2" x fabric width; cut into 32-8 1/2" A squares
- 9 H strips 8 1/2" x fabric width

PIECING THE BLOCKS

1. Draw a diagonal line from corner to corner on the wrong side of each B square.

2. Place one B square right sides together on one corner of a C square and stitch on the marked line (Diagram 1).

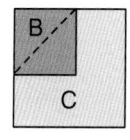

Diagram 1

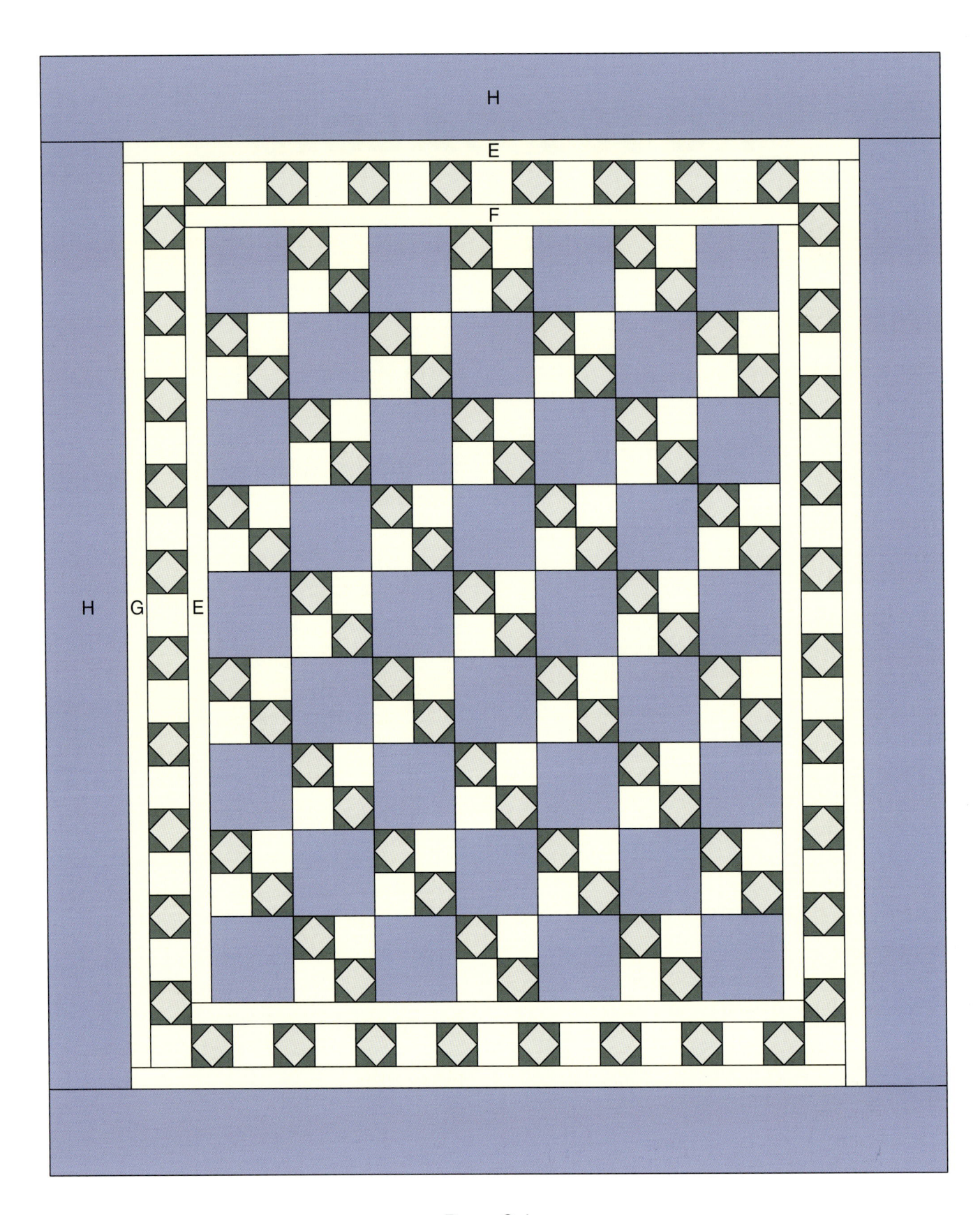

Roses Galore
Assembly Diagram 88" x 100"

ROSES GALORE

3. Trim the seam to $1/4"$; press B to the right side (Diagram 2).

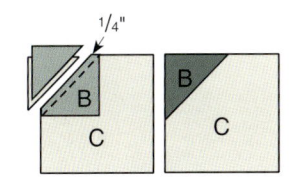

Diagram 2

4. Repeat with a B square on each corner of C to complete a B-C unit (Diagram 3); repeat for 98 B-C units. Set aside 36 units for borders.

Diagram 3

5. Sew a B-C unit to D (Diagram 4); press seam toward D. Repeat for 62 B-C-D units.

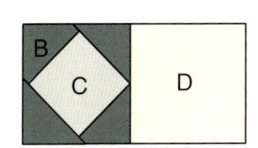

Diagram 4

6. Join two B-C-D units to complete one block (Diagram 5); repeat for 31 blocks. Press seams in one direction.

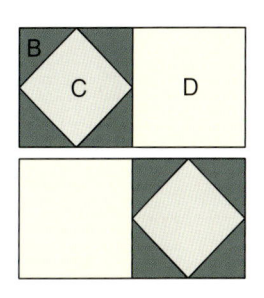

Diagram 5

ASSEMBLING THE TOP

1. Join four A squares and three pieced blocks to make a row (Diagram 6); repeat for five rows. Press seams toward A.

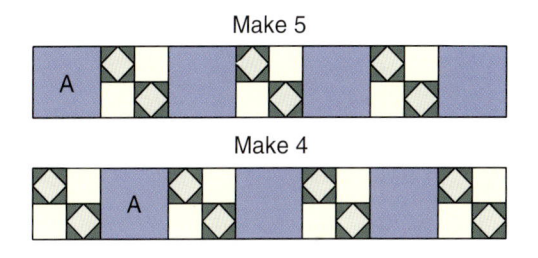

Make 5

Make 4

Diagram 6

2. Join four pieced blocks with three A squares to make a row (Diagram 6); repeat for four rows. Press seams toward A.

3. Join the rows referring to the Assembly Diagram; press seams in one direction.

4. Join the E/F/G strips on short ends to make one long strip. Cut four $72 1/2"$ E, two $60 1/2"$ F and two $84 1/2"$ G strips from the pieced strip.

5. Sew an E strip to opposite sides; press seams toward E. Sew an F strip to the top and bottom; press seams toward F.

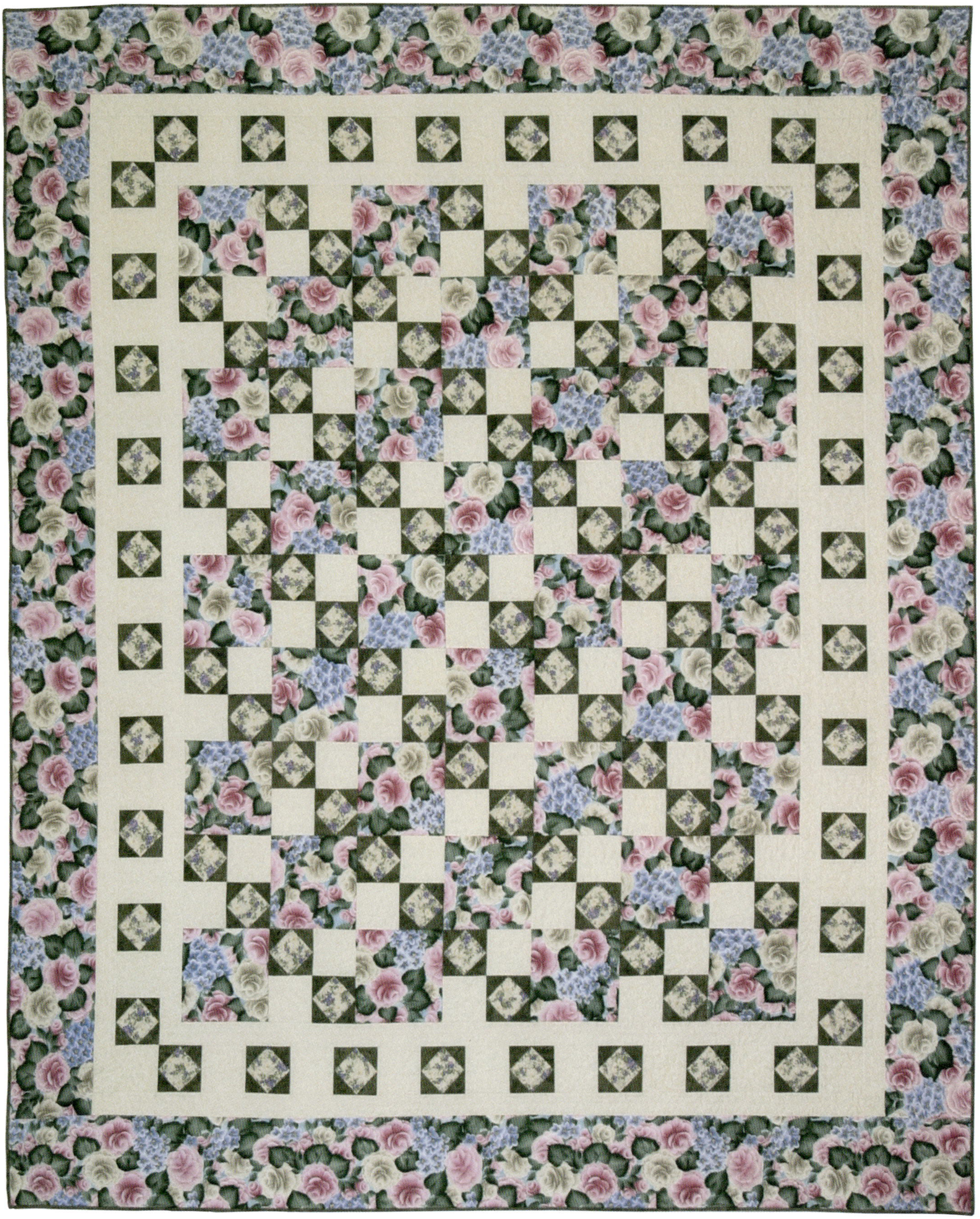

ROSES GALORE

6. Join 10 B-C units with nine D squares to make a pieced side row (Diagram 7); repeat for two side rows. Sew a side row to opposite sides of the pieced center; press seams toward E.

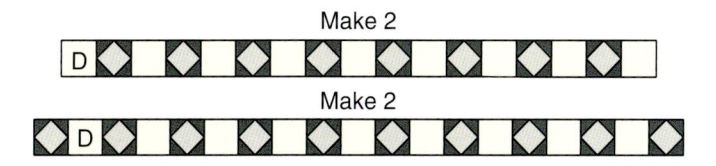

Make 2

Make 2

Diagram 7

7. Join eight B-C units with nine D squares to make a pieced top row (Diagram 7); repeat for the bottom row. Sew a row to the top and bottom of the pieced center; press seams toward F.

8. Sew a G strip to opposite sides and an E strip to the top and bottom of the pieced top; press seams toward strips.

9. Join the H strips on short ends to make one long strip; cut into four 88 1/2" H strips. Sew a strip to opposite sides and to the top and bottom; press seams toward H strips to complete the top.

FINISHING THE QUILT

1. Layer and baste quilt top for quilting method of choice referring to General Quiltmaking Instructions.

2. Quilt as desired.

3. Trim batting and backing even with top.

4. Bind quilt with green mottled binding strips referring to General Quiltmaking Instructions.

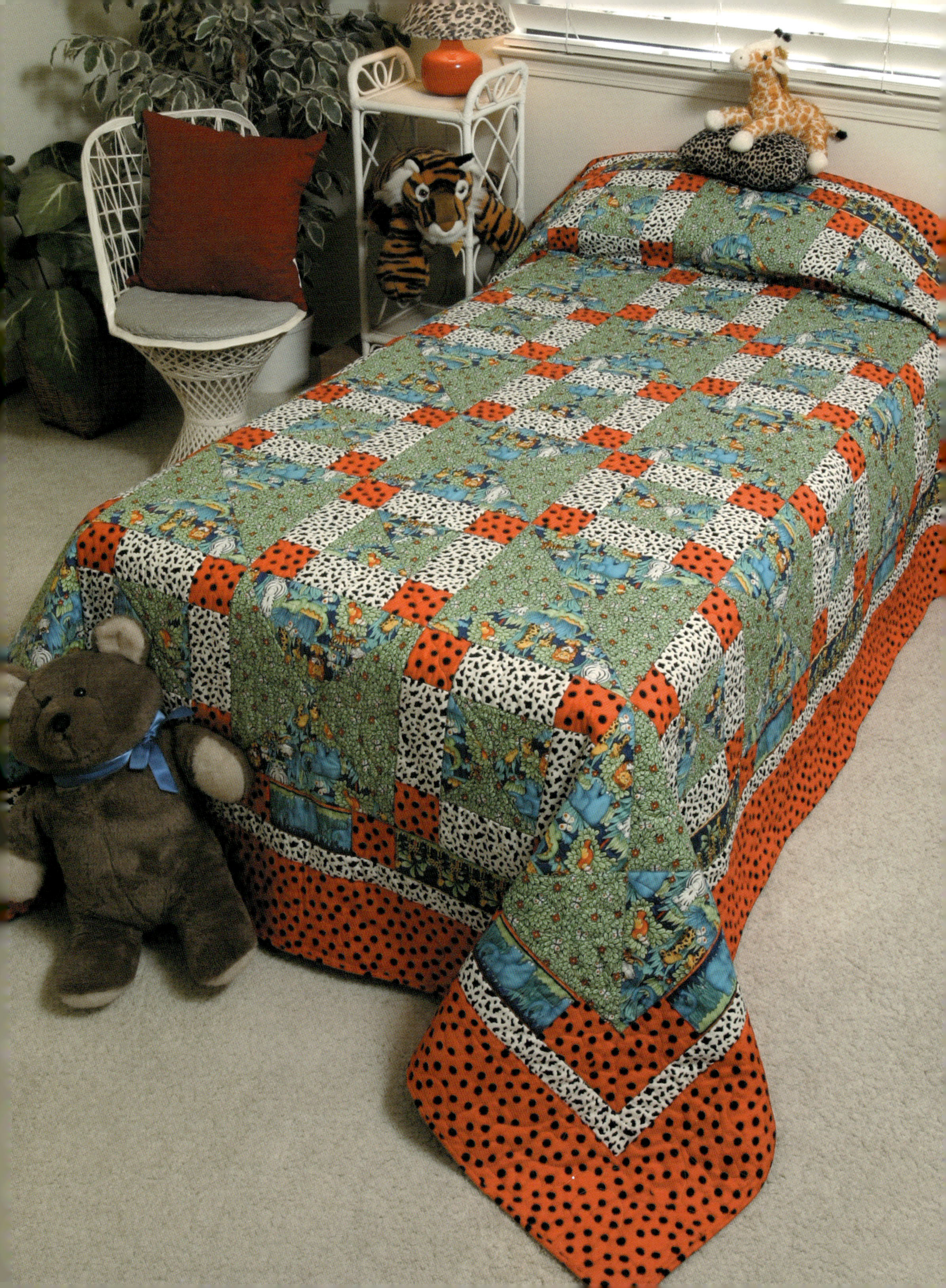

JUNGLE FEVER

Designed by Lee Grover

Finished Quilt Size 80" x 104"
Finished Block Size 12" x 12"
Number of Blocks 35

MATERIALS

Note: *All fabrics from the Jungle Safari collection from Northcott/Monarch*

Jungle stripe . . . . 1 1/2 yards
White zebra print . . . . 1 5/8 yards
Green print . . . . 1 2/3 yards
Animal print . . . . 1 2/3 yards

Note: *Fabric used was a directional print.*

Red-with-black dot . . . . 3 3/8 yards
Backing . . . . 86" x 110"
Batting. . . . . 86" x 110"
Coordinating thread
Rotary-cutting tools

CUTTING INSTRUCTIONS

Jungle stripe

Note: *Fabric used had a 3 1/2"-wide repeat stripe motif.*

Select a section of the stripe for G; cut the same section along length of stripe for G pieces. Repeat with a different section of the stripe for H pieces.
- 10-3 1/2" x 12 1/2" G rectangles
- 14-3 1/2" x 6 1/2" H rectangles

White zebra print
- 6 C strips 6 1/2" x fabric width; set aside 3 strips for C-D units. Cut the 3 remaining strips into 34-3 1/2" x 6 1/2" C rectangles
- 8 J/K strips 1 1/2" x fabric width

Green print
- 2 strips 7 1/4" x fabric width; cut into 9-7 1/4" squares. Cut each square on both diagonals to make 34 A triangles
- 3 strips 13 1/4" x fabric width; cut into 9-13 1/4" squares. Cut each square on both diagonals to make 36 F triangles

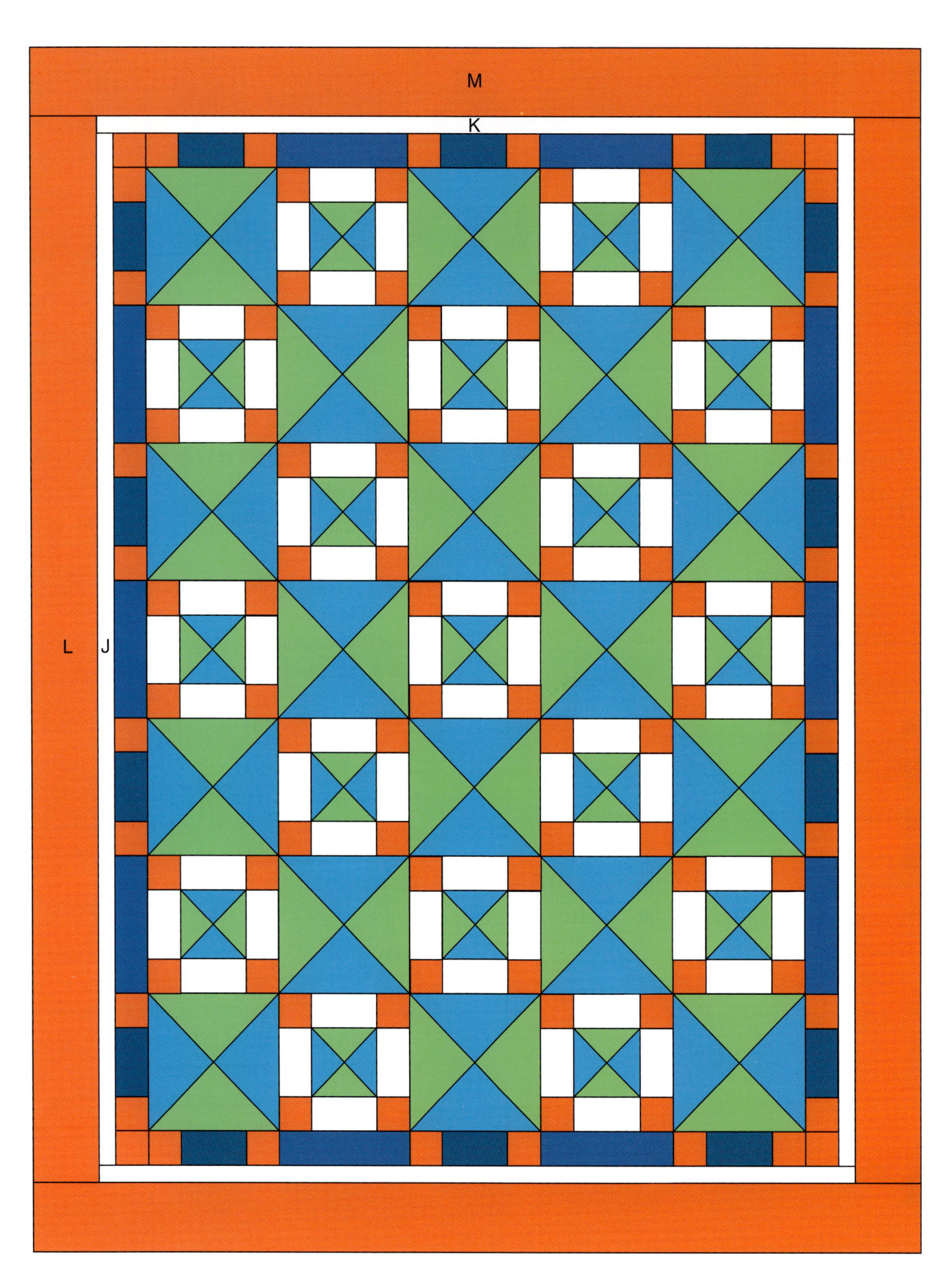

Jungle Fever
Assembly Diagram 80" x 104"

JUNGLE FEVER

Animal print

Note: Fabric used had a 3 1/2"-wide repeat stripe motif.

- 2 strips 7 1/4" x fabric width; cut into 9-7 1/4" squares. Cut each square on both diagonals to make 34 B triangles
- 3 strips 13 1/4" x fabric width; cut into 9 -13 1/4" squares. Cut each square on both diagonals to make 36 E triangles

Red-with-black dot

- 9 D strips 3 1/2" x fabric width; set aside 6 strips for C-D units. Cut the 3 remaining strips into 32-3 1/2" D squares.
- 9 L/M strips 6 1/2" x fabric width
- 10 strips 2 1/4" x fabric width for binding

PIECING THE X BLOCKS

1. If using a directional print for the E triangles, arrange the triangles in piles of each configuration, otherwise use E triangles in any order.

2. Arrange two E triangles with two F triangles (Diagram 1), noting direction of E.

Diagram 1

Sew an E triangle to F (Diagram 2); repeat. Press seams toward F.

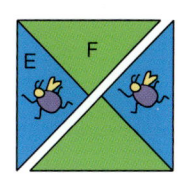

Diagram 2

3. Join the two E-F units to complete one X block (Diagram 3). Repeat for 18 X blocks.

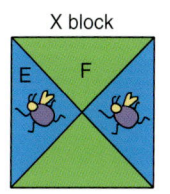

X block

Diagram 3

Note: You will have 10 blocks with E in the top and bottom positions and eight with E in the side positions (Diagram 4).

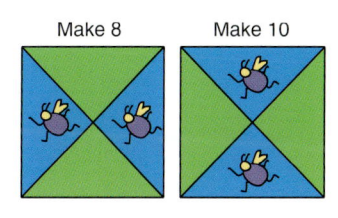

Make 8   Make 10

Diagram 4

PIECING THE Y BLOCKS

1. Prepare A-B center units as for E-F units in X blocks; repeat for 17 units.

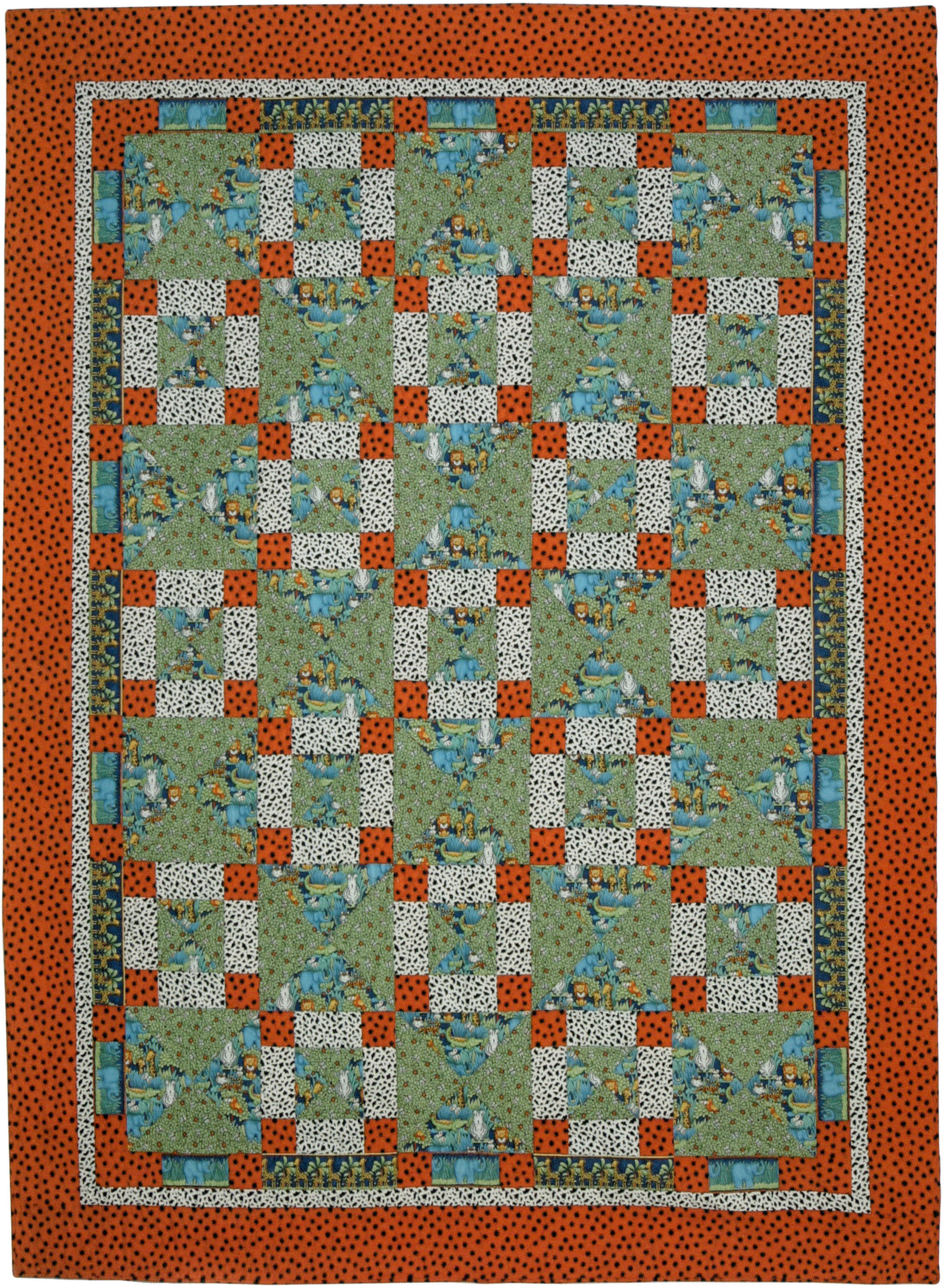

JUNGLE FEVER

2. Sew a C strip between two D strips with right sides together along length; press seams toward D. Repeat for three D-C-D strips. Cut strips into 34-3½" segments to make D-C-D units (Diagram 5).

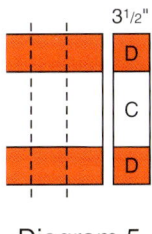

Diagram 5

3. Sew C to opposite sides of an A-B unit (Diagram 6); press seams toward C. Repeat for 17 units.

Diagram 6

4. Sew a D-C-D unit to an A-B-C unit to complete a Y block (Diagram 7); press seams toward D-C-D. Repeat for 17 Y blocks.

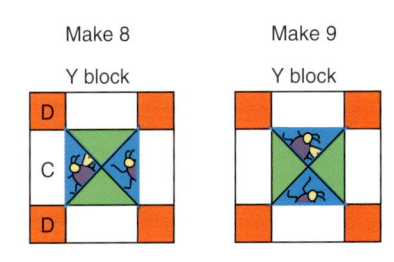

Make 8
Y block

Make 9
Y block

Diagram 7

ASSEMBLING THE TOP

1. Arrange three X blocks and two Y blocks and join to make a row (Diagram 8).

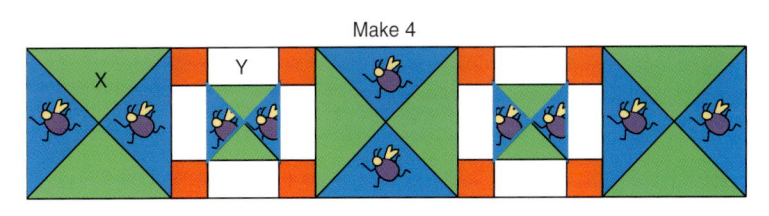

Make 4

Diagram 8

Note: If using directional prints, keep the A-B and E units in the upright positions. Repeat for four rows; press seams toward X blocks.

2. Arrange three Y blocks and two X blocks and join to make a row (Diagram 9) as in step 1. Repeat for three rows; press seams toward X blocks.

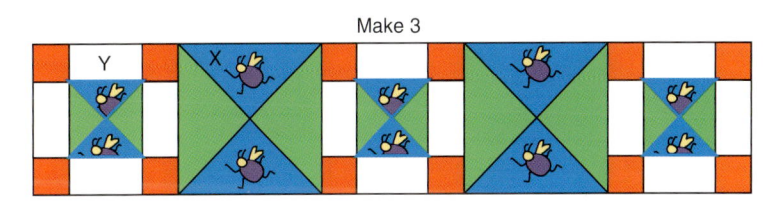

Make 3

Diagram 9

3. Join the rows referring to the Assembly Diagram for order; press seams in one direction.

JUNGLE FEVER

4. Join six D squares with two G and three H pieces (Diagram 10); press seams toward D. Repeat for two D-G-H strips.

Diagram 10

Note: G and H stripe pieces should be in the same upright position across the pieced strip.

5. Sew a D-G-H strip to the top and bottom of the pieced center; press seams toward strips.

6. Join 10 D squares with 3 G and four H pieces (Diagram 11); press seams toward D.

Diagram 11

7. Sew a D-G-H strip to opposite sides of the pieced center; press seams toward strips.

8. Join the J/K strips on short ends to make one long strip; cut into two 90 1/2" J strips and two 68 1/2" K strips. Sew a J strip to each long side and a K strip to the top and bottom of the pieced center; press seams toward strips.

9. Join L/M strips on short ends to make one long strip; cut into two 92 1/2" L strips and two 80 1/2" M strips. Sew an L strip to each long side and an M strip to the top and bottom of the pieced center; press seams toward strips.

FINISHING THE QUILT

1. Layer and baste quilt top for quilting method of choice referring to General Quiltmaking Instructions.

2. Quilt as desired.

3. Trim batting and backing even with top.

4. Bind quilt with red-with-black dot binding strips referring to General Quiltmaking Instructions.

STAR-CROSSED GARDEN

Designed by Christina Jensen

Finished Quilt Size 94" x 94"
Finished Block Size 12" x 12"
Number of Blocks 16

MATERIALS

Note: *All fabrics from the Hemingway collection from RJR Fabrics*

Large floral . . . . 1 1/2 yards
Green print . . . . 1 3/4 yards
Burgundy print . . . . 2 3/8 yards
Frond print . . . . 3 1/4 yards
Cream print . . . . 4 1/4 yards
Backing . . . . 100" x 100"
Batting . . . . 100" x 100"
Coordinating thread
Rotary-cutting tools

CUTTING INSTRUCTIONS

Large floral
- 16-9" x 9" A squares with floral motif centered in each square

Green print
- 7 strips 3 7/8" x fabric width; cut into 64-3 7/8" squares. Cut each square on 1 diagonal to make 128 C triangles
- 8 strips 3 1/2" x fabric width; cut into 96-3 1/2" F squares

Burgundy print
- 4 strips 6 1/2" x fabric width; cut into 24-6 1/2" D squares
- 8 strips 3 1/2" x fabric width; cut into 96-3 1/2" H squares
- 10 strips 2 1/4" x fabric width for binding

Frond print
- 2 strips 6 1/2" x fabric width; cut into 9-6 1/2" G squares
- 2 K strips 8 1/2" x 78 1/2" along length of fabric
- 2 L strips 8 1/2" x 94 1/2" along length of fabric

Cream print
- 6 strips 3 1/2" x fabric width; cut into 68-3 1/2" B squares
- 8 strips 6 1/2" x fabric width; cut into 96-3 1/2" x 6 1/2" E rectangles
- 2 I strips 3 1/2" x 66 1/2" along length of fabric
- 2 J strips 3 1/2" x 72 1/2" along length of fabric

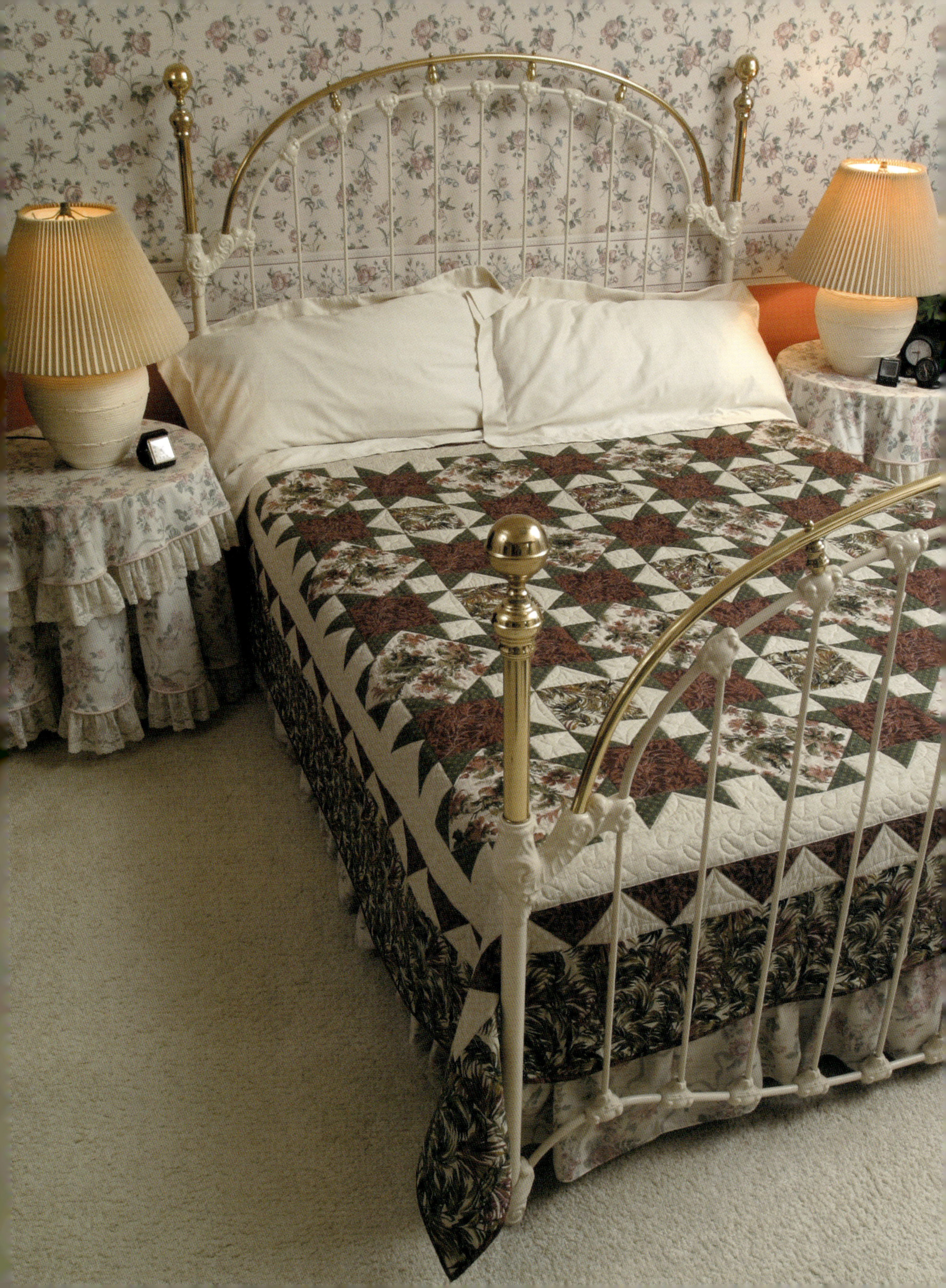

STAR-CROSSED GARDEN

PIECING THE BLOCKS AND SASHING UNITS

1. Sew a C triangle to two adjacent sides of a B square (Diagram 1); press seams toward B. Repeat to make 64 B-C units.

Diagram 1

2. Sew a B-C unit to each side of A to complete one block (Diagram 2); press seams toward A. Repeat to make 16 blocks.

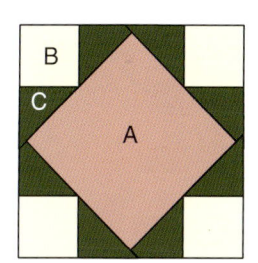

Diagram 2

3. Draw a diagonal line from corner to corner on the wrong side of each F square.

4. Place F on one end of E, stitch on the marked line, trim seam allowance to 1/4" and press F open (Diagram 3). Repeat on the opposite end of E to complete one F-E-F unit (Diagram 4).

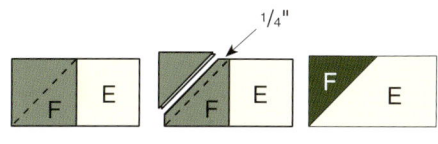

Diagram 3

Diagram 4

5. Repeat step 4 to make 48 F-E-F units.

6. Sew an F-E-F unit to opposite sides of D to complete one sashing unit (Diagram 5); press seams toward D. Repeat to make 24 sashing units.

Diagram 5

ASSEMBLING THE CENTER

Note: Refer to the Assembly Diagram as needed for the following instructions.

1. Join four blocks with three sashing units to make a block row (Diagram 6); repeat for four block rows. Press seams toward sashing units.

Diagram 6

45

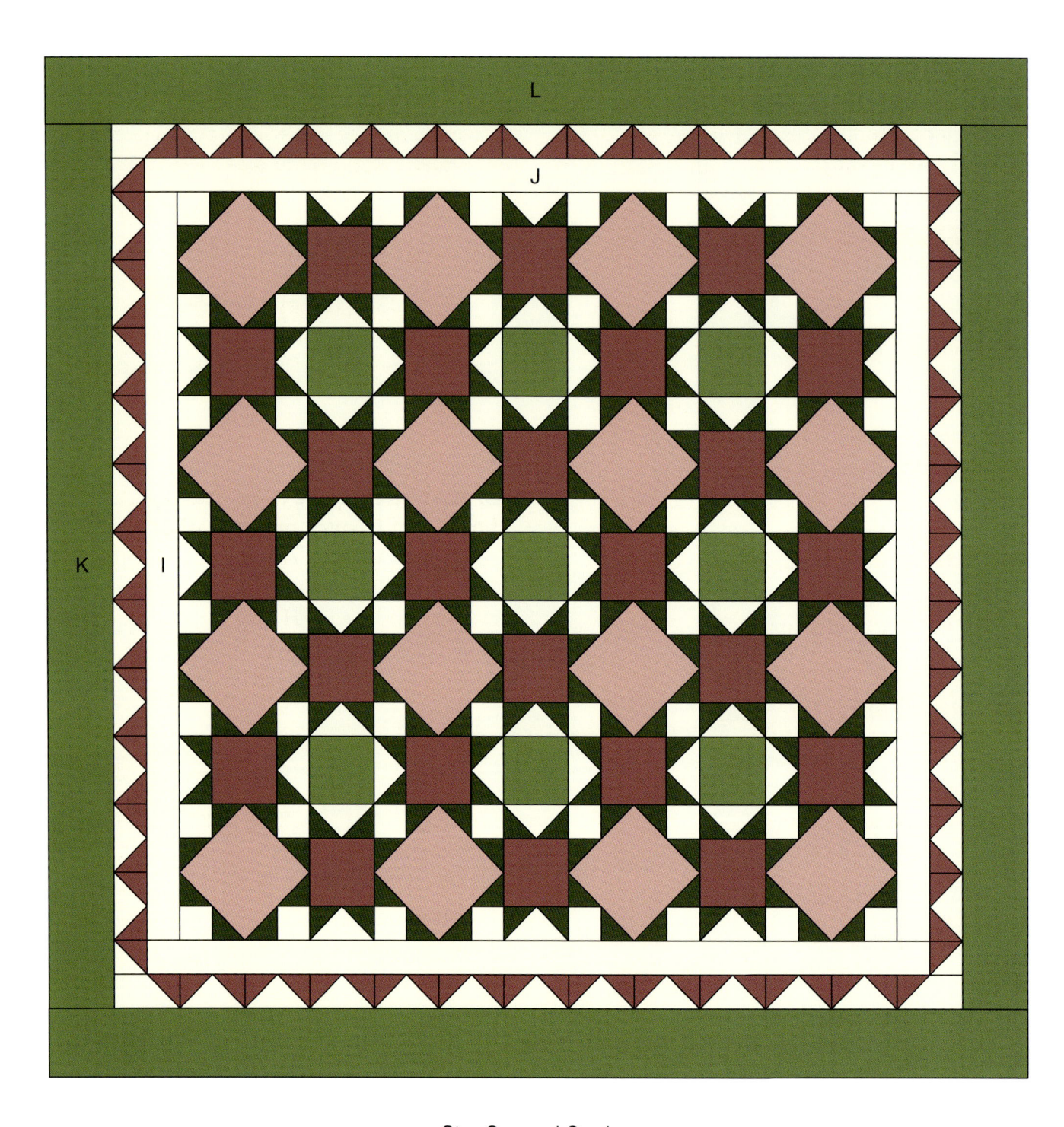

Star-Crossed Garden
Assembly Diagram 94" x 94"

STAR-CROSSED GARDEN

2. Join four sashing units with three G squares to make a sashing row (Diagram 7); repeat for three sashing rows. Press seams toward sashing units.

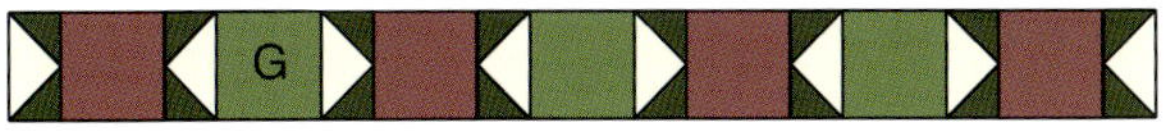

Diagram 7

3. Join the block rows with the sashing rows to complete the pieced center, beginning and ending with a block row.

ADDING THE BORDERS

Note: Refer to the Assembly Diagram as needed for the following instructions.

1. Sew an I strip to opposite sides and a J strip to the remaining sides of the pieced center; press seams toward strips.

2. Draw a diagonal line from corner to corner on the wrong side of each H square.

3. Refer to steps 3 and 4 of Piecing the Blocks and Sashing Units to complete one H-E-H unit (Diagram 8). Repeat to make 44 E-H units.

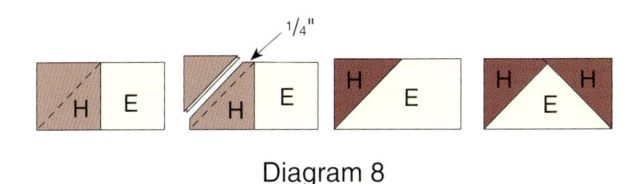

Diagram 8

4. Place an H square right sides together with a B square, stitch on the marked line, trim seam allowance to $1/4$" and press H open (Diagram 9); repeat to make four B-H units.

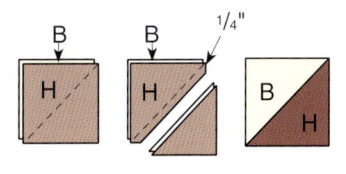

Diagram 9

5. Place an H square right sides together on one end of E, stitch on the marked line, trim seam allowance to $1/4$" and press H open (Diagram 10); repeat to make two E-H units and two reversed E-H units.

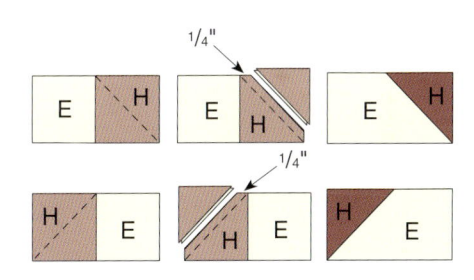

Diagram 10

6. Join 11 H-E-H units to make a strip (Diagram 11); press seams in one direction. Repeat to make four strips.

Diagram 11

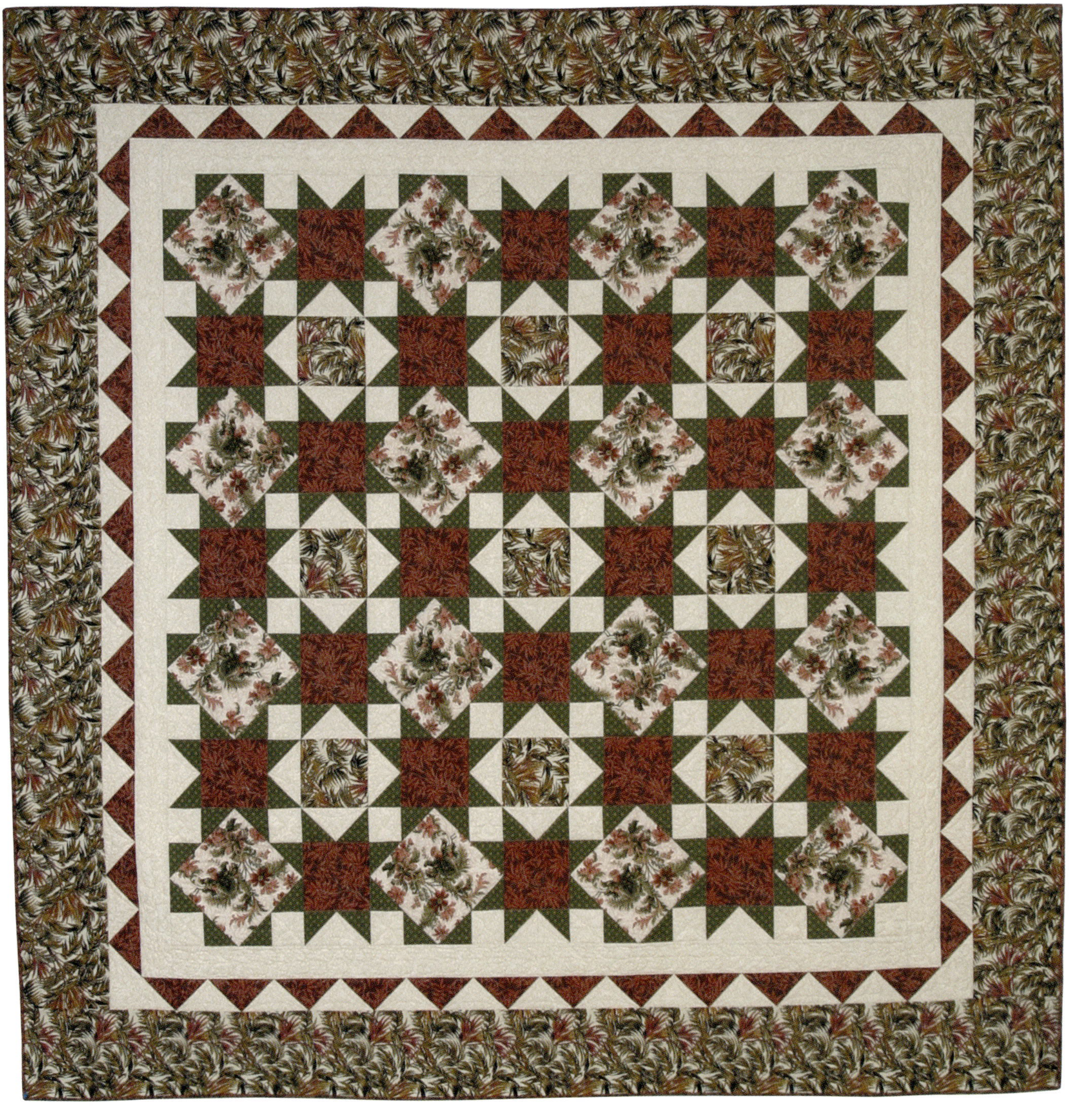

STAR-CROSSED GARDEN

7. Sew a B-H unit to each end of two strips (Diagram 12); sew a strip to opposite sides of the pieced center.

Diagram 12

8. Sew an E-H and reversed E-H unit to opposite ends of the remaining pieced strips (Diagram 13); sew a strip to the remaining sides of the pieced center.

Diagram 13

9. Sew a K strip to opposite sides and an L strip to the remaining sides to complete the top; press seams toward strips.

FINISHING THE QUILT

1. Layer and baste quilt top for quilting method of choice referring to General Quiltmaking Instructions.

2. Quilt as desired.

3. Trim batting and backing even with top.

4. Bind quilt with burgundy print binding strips referring to General Quiltmaking Instructions.

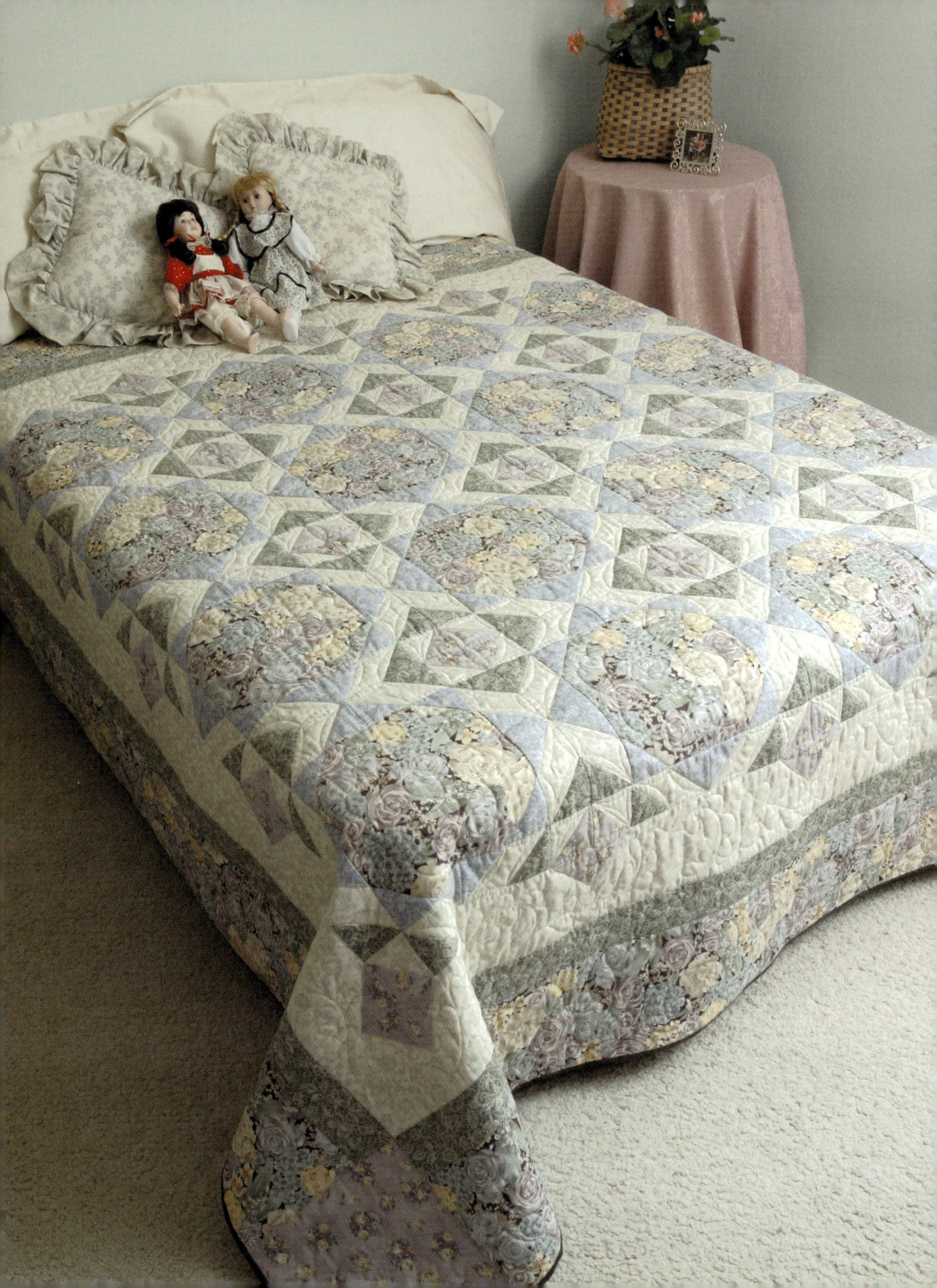

DIAMONDS & NOSEGAYS

Designed by Christina Jensen

Finished Quilt Size 90" x 90"
Finished Block Size 15" x 15"
Number of Blocks 16

MATERIALS

Note: All fabrics from the Wedded Bliss collection from Marcus Brothers

Dark green mottled. . . . . . . 3/4 yard
Lavender floral . . . . 1 1/8 yards
Blue print . . . . 1 3/8 yards
Green print . . . . 1 5/8 yards
Cream print . . . . 3 3/8 yards
Large floral . . . . 3 yards
Backing . . . . 96" x 96"
Batting. . . . . 96" x 96"
Coordinating thread
Rotary-cutting tools

CUTTING INSTRUCTIONS

Dark green mottled
- 10 strips 2 1/4" x fabric width for binding

Lavender floral
- 8 strips 3" x fabric width; cut into 100-3" E squares
- 1 strip 10 1/2" x fabric width; cut into 4-10 1/2" K squares

Blue print
- 14 strips 3" x fabric width; cut into 192-3" D squares

Green print
- 10 strips 3" x fabric width; cut into 128-3" C squares
- 7 I strips 3" x fabric width

Cream print
- 10 strips 5 1/2" x fabric width; cut into 128-3" x 5 1/2" B rectangles and 4-5 1/2" H squares
- 5 strips 3" x fabric width; cut into 64-3" F squares
- 3 strips 15 1/2" x fabric width; cut into 16-5 1/2" x 15 1/2" G rectangles

Large floral
- 4 strips 10 1/2" x fabric width; cut into 16-10 1/2" A squares
- 7 J strips 8" x fabric width

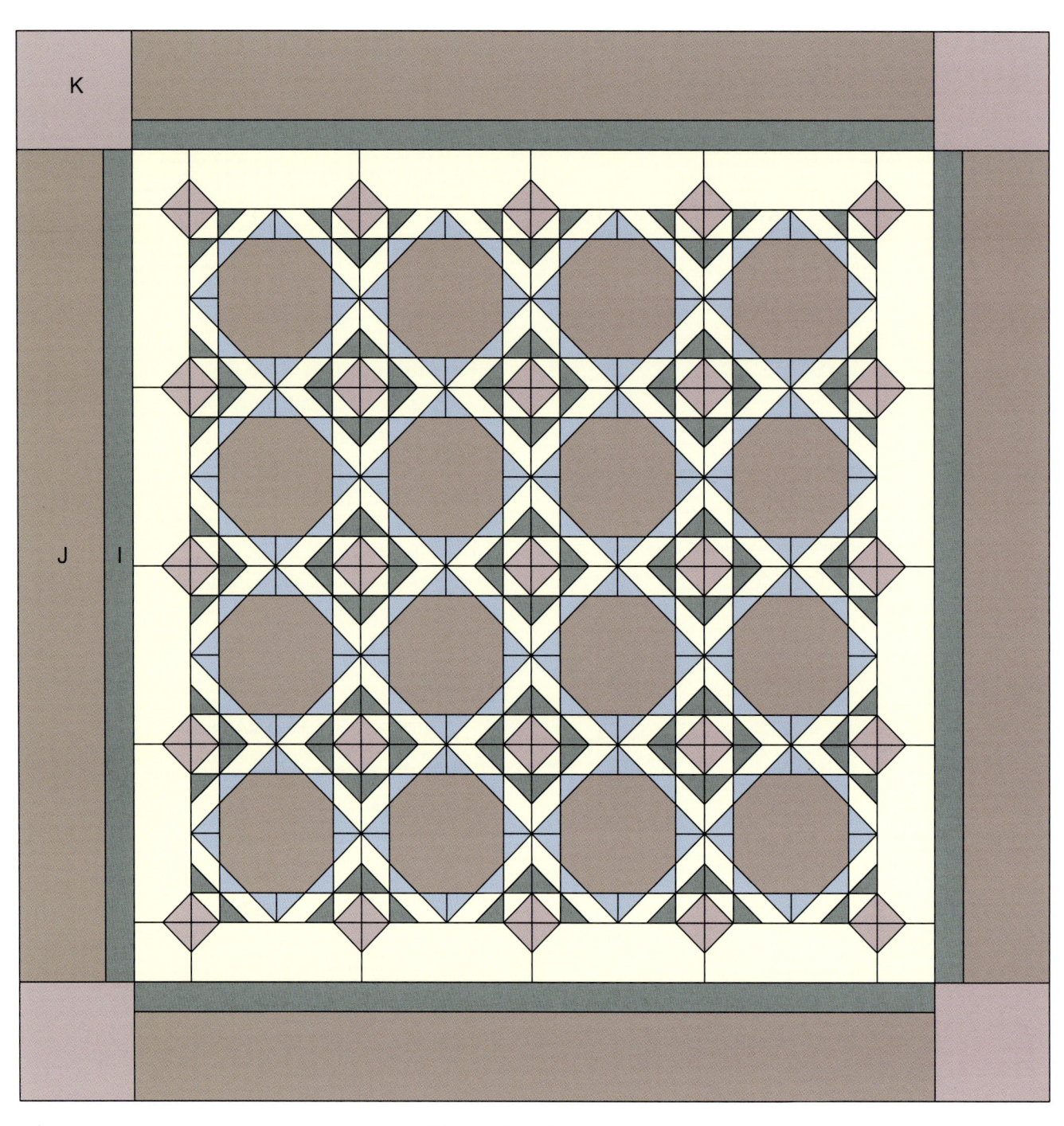

Diamonds & Nosegays
Assembly Diagram 90" x 90"

DIAMONDS & NOSEGAYS

PIECING UNITS

1. Draw a diagonal line from corner to corner on the wrong side of all C, D and E squares.

2. Place C right sides together on one end of B, stitch on the marked line, trim seam allowance to 1/4" and press C open (Diagram 1); repeat with D on the remaining end of B to complete one B-C-D unit (Diagram 2). Repeat to make 64 B-C-D units.

Diagram 1

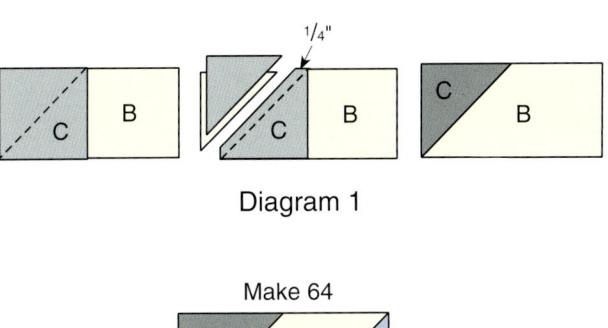

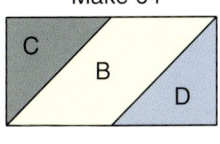

Diagram 2

3. Repeat step 2 to make 64 reversed B-C-D units (Diagram 3).

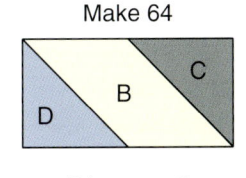

Diagram 3

4. Place E right sides together with F, stitch on the marked line, trim seam allowance to 1/4" and press E open (Diagram 4); repeat to make 64 E-F units.

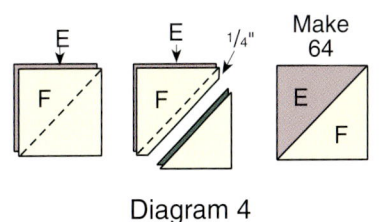

Diagram 4

5. Place D right sides together on each corner of A, stitch on the marked lines, trim seam allowances to 1/4" and press D open (Diagram 5); repeat to make 16 A-D units.

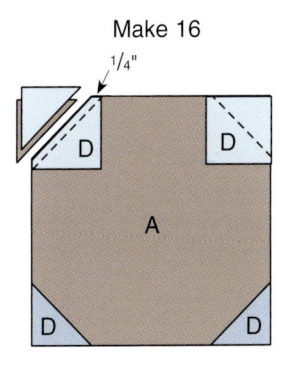

Diagram 5

6. Place E right sides together on two corners of G, stitch on the marked lines, trim seam allowances to 1/4" and press E open (Diagram 6); repeat to make 16 E-G units.

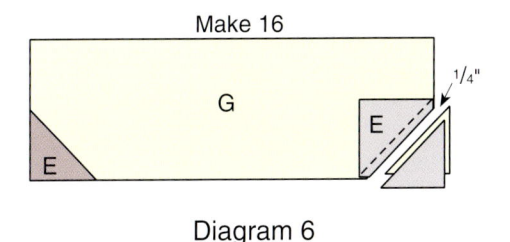

Diagram 6

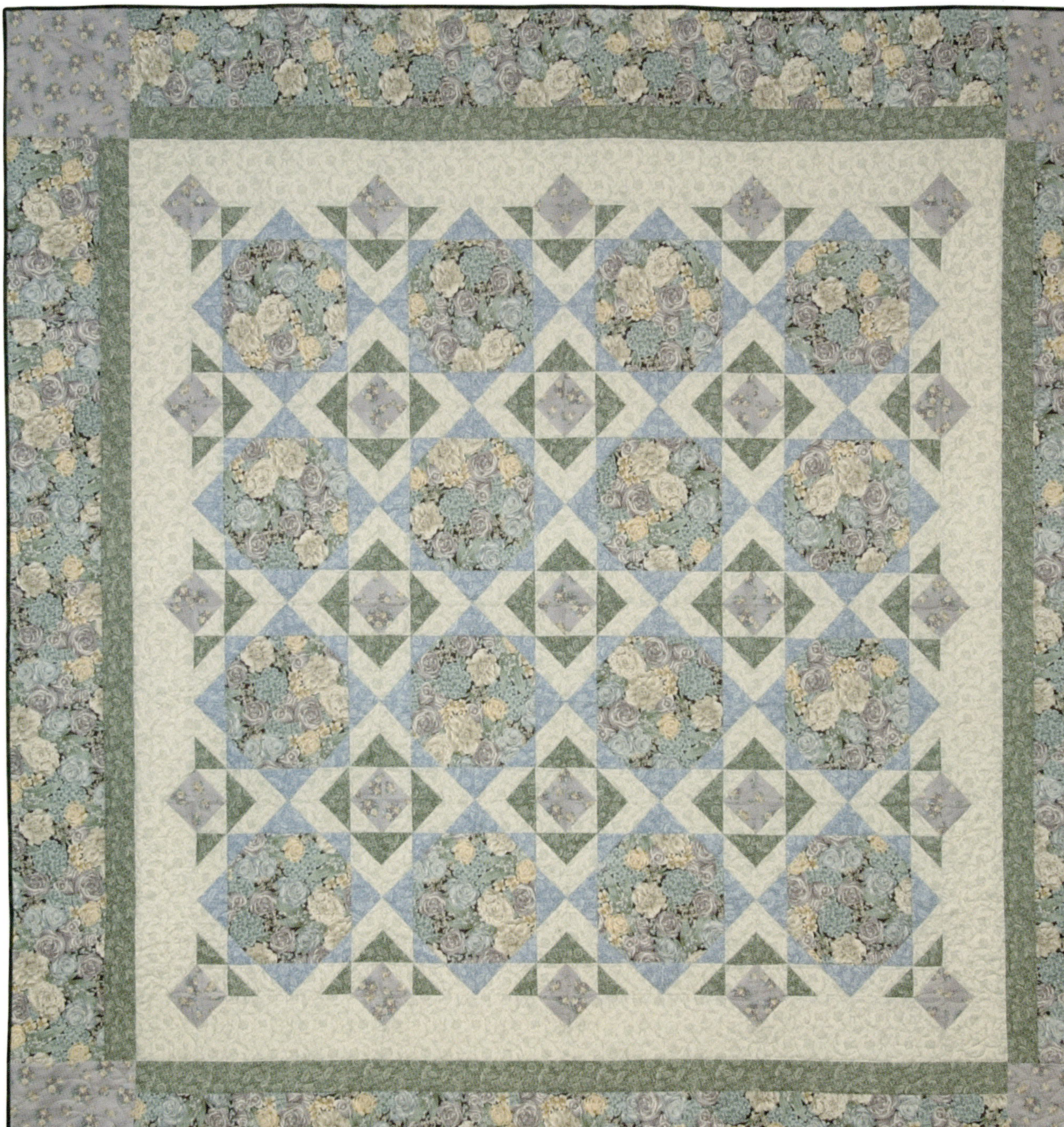

DIAMONDS & NOSEGAYS

7. Place E right sides together on one corner of H, stitch on the marked line, trim seam allowance to 1/4" and press E open (Diagram 7); repeat to make four E-H units.

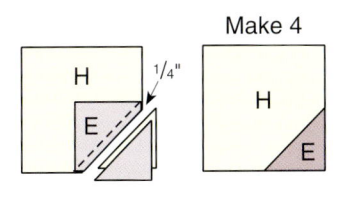

Diagram 7

COMPLETING THE BLOCKS

1. Join a B-C-D unit with a reversed B-C-D unit on the blue ends (Diagram 8); press seam toward B-C-D. Repeat to make 64 B-C-D strips.

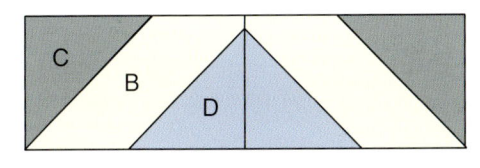

Diagram 8

2. Sew a B-C-D strip to opposite sides of A-D (Diagram 9); press seams toward A-D. Repeat with all A-D units.

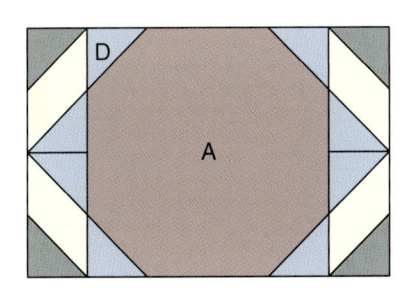

Diagram 9

3. Sew E-F to each end of the remaining B-C-D strips (Diagram 10); press seams toward E-F.

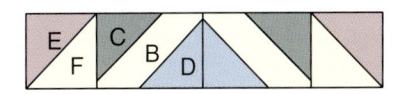

Diagram 10

4. Sew a pieced strip to the remaining sides of the A-D units to complete 16 blocks (Diagram 11); press seams toward the pieced strips.

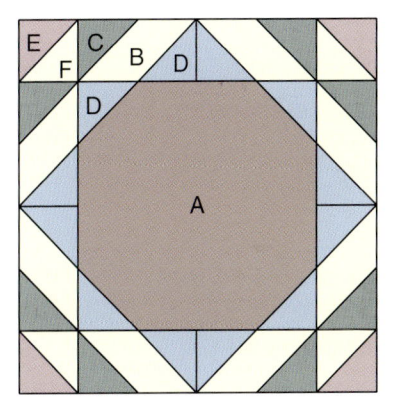

Diagram 11

ASSEMBLING THE TOP

Note: Refer to the Assembly Diagram as needed for the following instructions.

1. Join four blocks to make a row (Diagram 12); press seams in one direction. Repeat for four rows; join the rows to complete the pieced center. Press seams in one direction.

DIAMONDS & NOSEGAYS

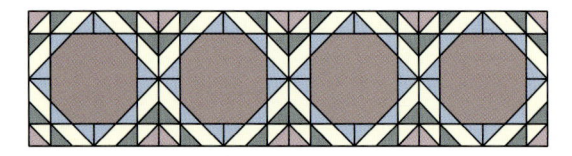

Diagram 12

2. Join four E-G units on short ends (Diagram 13); press seams in one direction. Repeat to make four strips.

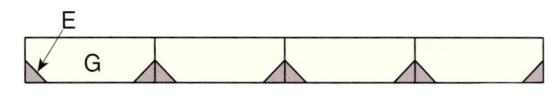

Diagram 13

3. Sew a strip to opposite sides of the pieced center, aligning E corners with E block corners on each side; press seams toward strips.

4. Sew E-H to each end of the remaining E-G strips (Diagram 14); press seams toward E-G strips. Sew a strip to the remaining sides of the pieced center; press seams toward strips.

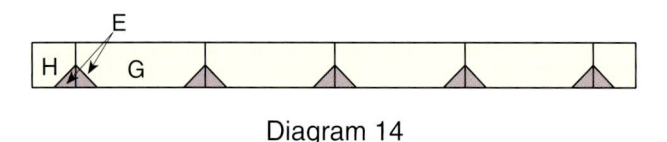

Diagram 14

5. Join I strips on short ends to make a long strip; cut into four 70 1/2" I strips.

6. Join J strips on short ends to make a long strip; cut into four 70 1/2" J strips.

7. Sew an I strip to a J strip along length; press seam toward J. Repeat to make four I-J strips.

8. Sew a strip to opposite sides of the pieced center; press seams toward strips.

9. Sew K to each end of the remaining I-J strips; press seams toward I-J strips. Sew a strip to the remaining sides; press seams toward strips to complete the top.

FINISHING THE QUILT

1. Layer and baste quilt top for quilting method of choice referring to General Quiltmaking Instructions.

2. Quilt as desired.

3. Trim batting and backing even with top.

4. Bind quilt with dark green mottled binding strips referring to General Quiltmaking Instructions.

GENERAL QUILTMAKING INSTRUCTIONS

In order to make a quilt in seven days you will need to follow some fast quiltmaking techniques that are discussed in this section. Of course, if you prefer, you can use traditional methods. But keep in mind your quilt will probably take more than seven days.

FABRIC

For several hundred years, quilts were made with 100% cotton fabric, and this remains today the fabric of choice for most quilters.

There are many properties in cotton that make it especially well suited to quiltmaking. There is less distortion in cotton fabric, thereby affording the quilter greater security in making certain that even the smallest bits of fabric will fit together. Because a quilt block made of cotton can be ironed flat with a steam iron, a puckered area, created by mistake, can be fixed. The sewing machine needle can move through cotton with a great deal of ease when compared to some synthetic fabrics. While you may find that quilt artists today often use other kinds of fabric, to make these quilts quickly and accurately, 100% cotton is strongly recommended.

For years, quilters were advised to prewash all of their fabric to test for colorfastness and shrinkage. Now most quilters don't bother to prewash all of their fabric, but they do pre-test. Cut a strip about 2" wide from each piece of fabric that you will use in your quilt. Measure both the length and the width of the strip. Then immerse the strip in a bowl of very hot water, using a separate bowl for each piece of fabric.

Be especially concerned about reds and dark blues because they have a tendency to bleed if the initial dyeing was not done correctly. If it's one of your favorite fabrics that's bleeding, you might be able to salvage the fabric. Try washing the fabric in very hot water until you've washed out all of the excess dye. Unfortunately, fabrics that continue to bleed after they have been washed repeatedly will bleed forever. So, eliminate them right at the start.

Now, take each one of the strips and iron them dry using a hot iron. Be especially careful not to stretch the strip. When the strips are completely dry, measure and compare them to your original strip. If all of your fabric is shrinking the same amount, you don't have to worry about uneven shrinkage in your quilt. When you wash the final quilt, the puckering that will result will give you the look of an antique quilt. If you don't want this look, you are going to have to wash and dry all of your fabric before you start cutting. Iron the fabric, using some spray starch or sizing to give the fabric a crisp finish.

If you are never planning to wash your quilt, i.e. your quilt is intended to be a wall hanging, you could eliminate the pre-testing process. You may run the risk, however, of some future relative to whom you have willed your quilts deciding that the wall hanging needs freshening by washing.

Before beginning to work, make sure that your fabric is absolutely square. If it is not, you will have difficulty cutting square pieces. Fabric is woven with crosswise and lengthwise threads. Lengthwise threads should be parallel to the selvage (that's the finished edge along the sides; sometimes the fabric company prints its name along the selvage), and crosswise threads should be perpendicular to the selvage. If fabric is off grain, you can usually straighten it by pulling gently on the true bias in the opposite direction to the off-grain edge. Continue doing this until the crosswise threads are at a right angle to the lengthwise threads.

GENERAL QUILTMAKING INSTRUCTIONS

ROTARY CUTTING

The introduction of the rotary cutter in the late 1970's has made all the difference in quilt making today. With rotary cutting you can make quilts faster and with greater accuracy. With rotary cutting, traditional quilt templates are not used. Instead, the pieces are cut into strips and then the strips are cut into other shapes.

For rotary cutting, you will need three important tools: a rotary cutter, a mat and an acrylic ruler. There are currently many different brands and types on the market. Choose the ones that you feel will work for you.

There are several different rotary cutters now available with special features that you might prefer, such as the type of handle, whether the cutter can be used for both right- and left-handed quilters, safety features, size, and finally the cost.

Don't attempt to use the rotary cutter without an accompanying protective mat. The mat will not only protect your table from becoming scratched, but it will protect your cutter as well. Most mats are self-healing and will not dull the cutting blades. Mats are available in many sizes, but if this is your first attempt at rotary cutting, an 18" x 24" mat is probably your best choice. When you are not using your mat, be sure that it is left on a flat surface. Otherwise your mat will bend. If you want to keep your mat from warping, make certain that it is not placed in direct sunlight; the heat can cause the mat to warp. You won't be able cut accurately when you use a bent or warped mat.

A must for cutting accurate strips is a strong straight edge. Acrylic rulers are the perfect choice for this. There are many different acrylic rulers on the market, and they come in several widths and lengths. Either a 6" x 24" or a 6" x 12" ruler will be the most useful. The longer ruler will allow you to fold your fabric only once while the smaller size will require folding the fabric twice. Make sure that your ruler has $1/8$" increment markings in both directions plus a 45-degree marking.

CUTTING STRIPS

Before beginning to work, iron your fabric to remove the wrinkles. Fold the fabric in half, lengthwise, bringing the selvage edges together. Fold in half again. Make sure that there are no wrinkles in the fabric.

Now place the folded fabric on the cutting mat. Place the fabric length on the right side if you are right handed or on the left side if you are left-handed. The fold of the fabric should line up along one of the grid lines printed on the mat.

If you are right handed:

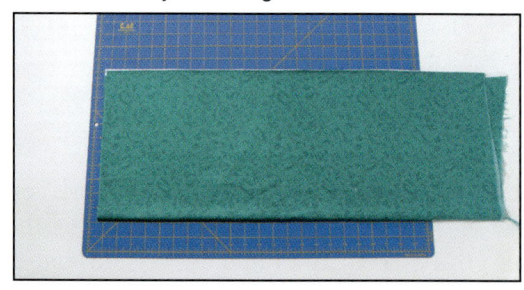

If you are left handed:

Lay the acrylic ruler on the mat near the cut edge; the ruler markings should be even with the grid on the mat. Hold the ruler firmly with your left hand (or, with your right hand if you are left-handed). To provide extra stability, keep your small finger on the mat. Now hold the rotary cutter with the blade against the ruler and cut away from you in one quick motion.

Place the ruler on the required width line along the cut edge of the fabric and cut the strip, making sure that you always cut away from you. Cut the number of strips called for in the directions.

After you have cut a few strips, you will want to check to make certain that your fabric continues to be perfectly square. If necessary, you should re-square the fabric. If you fail to do this, your strips may be bowed with a "v" in the center, causing your piecing to become inaccurate as you continue working.

CUTTING SQUARES AND RECTANGLES

Place a stack of strips on the cutting mat. You will be more successful in cutting—at least in the beginning—if you work with no more than four strips at a time. Make certain that the strips are lined up very evenly. Following the instructions given for the quilt, cut the required number of blocks or rectangles.

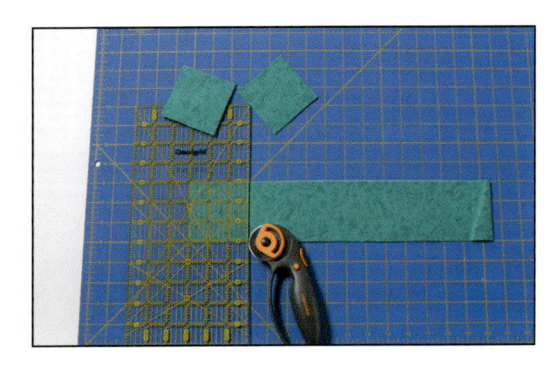

CUTTING TRIANGLES

There are a number of different triangle constructions used in these quilts including Half-Square Triangles, Quarter-Square Triangles, and Triangle Squares.

The short sides of a Half-Square Triangle are on the straight grain of the fabric. This is especially necessary if the short edges are on the outer side of the block. Cut the squares the size indicated in the instructions, then cut the square in half diagonally.

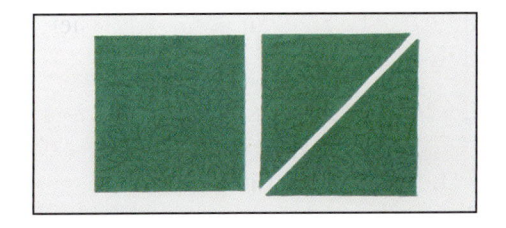

GENERAL QUILTMAKING INSTRUCTIONS

Quarter-Square Triangles are used when the long edge of the triangle must be on the straight grain. This is important when the long edge is on the outside edge of the block. Again, cut the squares the proper size; then cut diagonally into quarters.

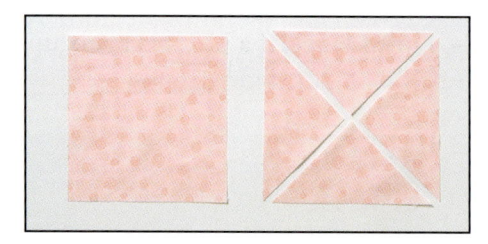

Triangle Squares are squares made up of two different-colored triangles. To make these squares, you can cut individual triangles as described in Half-Square Triangles. Then sew two triangles together. A quick method, especially if you have several triangle squares with the same fabric, is to sew two squares together. Draw a diagonal line on the wrong side of the lighter square. Place two squares right sides together and sew 1/4" from each side of the drawn line. Cut along the drawn line, and you have created two Triangle Squares.

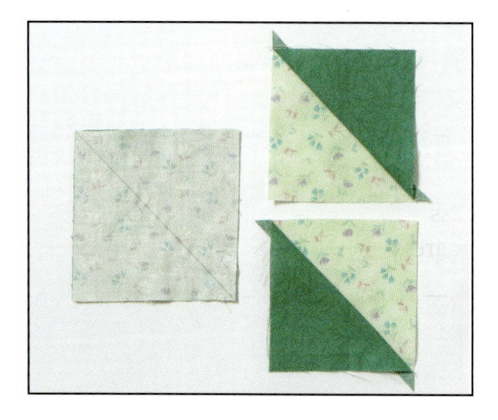

STITCH AND FLIP

This is a method for quickly creating triangles and octagons or trapezoids. Instead of cutting these shapes, you cut and sew squares or rectangles together.

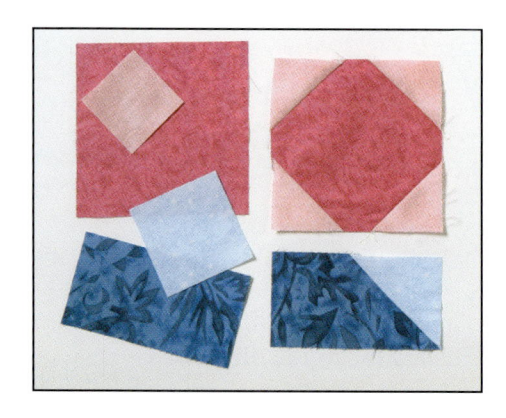

With right sides together, a small square is placed in the corner of a larger square or rectangle. You then sew diagonally from corner to corner of the small square.

Trim the corner about 1/4" from the seam line.

Flip the triangle over and iron.

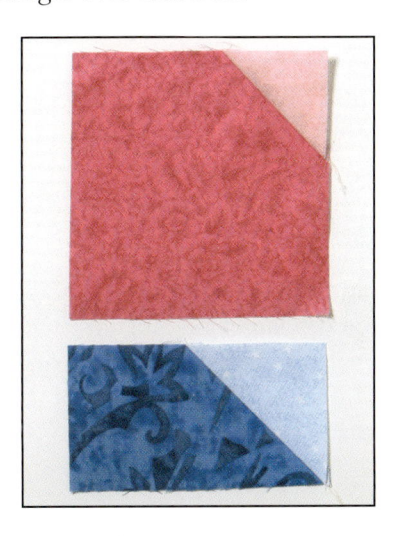

Repeat at the other corners according to individual pattern instructions.

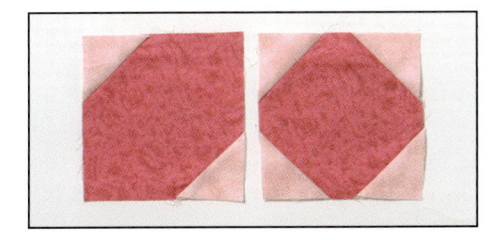

STRIP PIECING

Most of the quilts in this book are done using the strip piecing technique. This is a much faster and easier method of making quilts rather than creating the blocks piece by piece. With this method, two or more strips are sewn together then cut at certain intervals. For instance, if a block is made up of several 3" squares, cut 3"-wide strips along the crosswise grain.

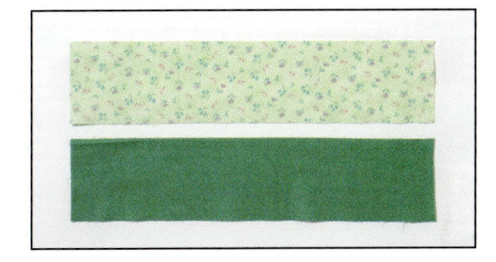

With right sides together, sew two strips along the length. The seam should be pressed toward the dark side of the fabric.

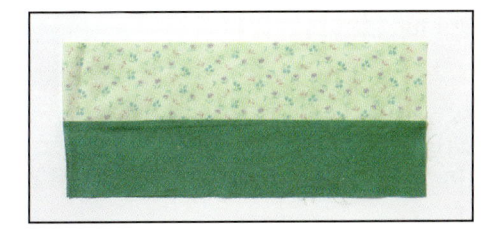

Cut across strips at 3 1/2" intervals to create pairs of 3 1/2" squares.

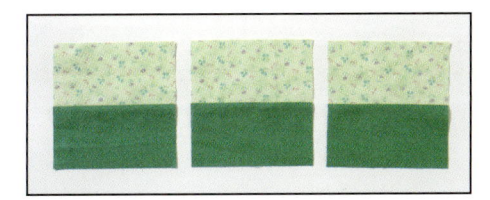

GENERAL QUILTMAKING INSTRUCTIONS

CHAIN PIECING

Another quick technique to enable you to finish these quilts in seven days (or less!) is chain piecing. This technique is used when sewing several of the same shapes together. If you want to sew several triangles together, place the first two with their right sides together and sew along the longest edge. Do not begin and end your thread with each triangle, but let the thread run over a continuous chain of triangles. When you have made a row of triangles, snip them apart. Don't worry about the threads coming undone; they will eventually be anchored by the cross seams.

ADDING BORDERS

Borders are usually added to the top, sides and bottom of a quilt.

To add your borders, measure the quilt top lengthwise through the center and cut two border strips to that length by the width measurement given in the instructions. Sew both strips to the sides of the quilt.

Now measure the quilt top crosswise through the center, being sure to include the measurement of the borders you have just added. Cut two border strips, following the width measurement given in the instructions. Instructions for each quilt include the precise sizes of all borders needed to complete the quilt top if all sewing is accurate.

Add these borders to the top and bottom of the quilt. Repeat this process for any additional borders. Use a 1/4" seam allowance at all times and press all of the seams to the darker side. Press the quilt top carefully,

ATTACHING THE BATTING AND BACKING

There are a number of different types of batting on the market today including the new fusible battings that eliminate the need for basting. Your choice of batting will depend upon how you are planning to use your quilt. If you quilt is to serve as a wall hanging, you will probably want to use a thin cotton batting. Batting made with a thin cotton or cotton/polyester blend works best for machine quilting. Very thick polyester batting should be used only for tied quilts.

The best fabric for quilt backing is 100% cotton fabric. If your quilt is larger than the available fabric you will have to piece your backing fabric. When joining the fabric, try not to have a seam going down the center. Instead cut off the selvages and make a center strip that is about 36" wide and have narrower strips at the sides. Seam the pieces together and carefully iron the seams open. (This is one of the few times in making a quilt that a seam should be pressed open.) Several fabric manufacturers are now selling fabric in 90" or 108"-widths for use as backing fabric.

The batting and the backing should be cut about one to two inches larger on all sides than the quilt top. Place the backing wrong side up on a flat surface. Smooth out the batting on top of this, matching the outer edges. Center the quilt top, right side up, on top of the batting.

Now the quilt layers must be held together before quilting, and there are several methods for doing this:

Thread Basting Baste the three layers together with long stitches. Start in the center and sew toward the edges in a number of diagonal lines.

Safety-pin Basting Starting from the center and working toward the edges, pin through all layers at one time with large safety pins. The pins should be placed no more than 4" apart. As you work, think of your quilting plan to make sure that the pins will avoid prospective quilting lines.

Quilt-gun Basting This handy trigger tool pushes nylon tags through all layers of the quilt. Start in the center and work toward the outside edges. The tags should be placed about 4" apart. You can sew right over the tags, which can then be easily removed by cutting them off with scissors.

Spray or Heat-Set Basting Several manufacturers have spray adhesives available especially for quilters. Apply these products by following the manufacturers' directions. You might want to test these products before you use them to make sure that they meet your requirements.

Fusible Iron-on Batting These battings are a wonderful new way to hold quilt layers together without using any of the other time-consuming methods of basting. Again, you will want to test these battings to be certain that you are happy with the results. Follow the manufacturers' directions.

QUILTING

If you like the process of hand quilting, you can—of course—finish these projects by hand quilting. However, if you want to finish these quilts in seven days, you may have to use a sewing machine for quilting.

If you have never used a sewing machine for quilting, you may want to find a book and read about the technique. You do not need a special machine for quilting. Just make sure that your machine has been oiled and is in good working condition.

If you are going to do machine quilting, you should invest in an even-feed foot. This foot is designed to feed the top and bottom layers of a quilt evenly through the machine. The foot prevents puckers from forming as you machine quilt. Use a fine transparent nylon thread in the top and regular sewing thread in the bobbin.

"Quilting in the ditch" is one of the easiest ways to machine quilt.

This is a term used to describe stitching along the seam line between two pieces of fabric. Using your fingers, pull the blocks or pieces apart slightly and machine stitch right between the two pieces. The stitching will look better if you keep the stitching to the side of the seam that does not have the extra bulk of the seam allowance under it. The quilting will be hidden in the seam.

Free-form machine quilting can be used to quilt around a design or to quilt a motif. The quilting is done with a darning foot and the feed dogs down on the sewing machine. It takes practice to master Free-form quilting because you are controlling the movement of the quilt under the needle rather than the sewing machine moving the quilt. You can quilt in any direction—up and down, side to side and even in circles—without pivoting the quilt around the needle. Practice this quilting method before trying it on your quilt.

ATTACHING THE CONTINUOUS MACHINE BINDING

Once the quilt has been quilted, the edges must be bound. Start by trimming the backing and batting even with the quilt top. Measure the quilt top and cut enough 2¼" wide strips to go around all four sides of the quilt plus 12". Join the strips end to end with diagonal seams and trim the corners

GENERAL QUILTMAKING INSTRUCTIONS

Press the seams open. Cut one end of the strip at a 45-degree angle and press under ¼".

Press entire strip in half lengthwise, wrong sides together.

On the front of the quilt, position the binding in the middle of one side, keeping the raw edges together. Sew the binding to the quilt with the ¼" seam allowance, beginning about three inches below the folded end of the binding.

At the corner, stop ¼" from the edge of the quilt and backstitch.

Fold binding away from quilt so it is at a right angle to edge just sewn. Then, fold the binding back on itself so the fold is on the quilt edge and the raw edges are aligned with the adjacent side of the quilt. Begin sewing at the quilt edge.

Continue in the same way around the remaining sides of the quilt. Stop about 2" away from the starting point. Trim any excess binding and tuck it inside the folded end. Finish the stitching.

Fold the binding to the back of the quilt so the seam line is covered; hand-stitch the binding in place on the backside of the quilt.

After you have finished making your quilt, Always sign and date your quilt when finished. You can make a label by cross stitching or embroidering or even writing on a label or on the back of your quilt with a permanent marking pen. If you are friends with your computer, you can even create an attractive label on the computer.